Growth

Structural Change

ECONOMICS TODAY
Edited by Andrew Leake

The *Economics Today* series surveys contemporary headline topics in applied economics. Each book in the series is written by an expert in the field in a style that is fluently readable. It serves the student of introductory economic principles while also making the subject accessible to a more general reader. The series embraces the problem-solving skills of the new generation of students and stresses the importance of real-world issues and the significance of economic ideas.

* * *

Published

Andrew Leake: **The Economic Question**
Jean-Louis Barsoux and Peter Lawrence: **The Challenge of British Management**
Andy Beharell: **Unemployment and Job Creation**
Frank Burchill: **Labour Relations**
Mark Cook and Nigel M. Healey: **Growth and Structural Change**
Kenneth Durham: **The New City**
S.F. Goodman: **The European Community** (2nd edition)
Kent Matthews: **Macroeconomics and the Market**
Charles Smith: **Economic Development, Growth and Welfare**
Jenny Wales: **Investigating Social Issues**
John Wigley and Carol Lipman: **The Enterprise Economy**
Margaret Wilkinson: **Taxation**

Forthcoming

Ian Hodge: **Environmental Economics**
John Wigley: **The Rebirth of Russia**

Series Standing Order
If you would like to receive future titles in this series as they are published, you can make use of our standing order facility. To place a standing order please contact your bookseller or, in case of difficulty, write to us at the address below with your name and address and the name of the series. Please state with which title you wish to begin your standing order. (If you live outside the United Kingdom we may not have the rights for your area, in which case we will forward your order to the publisher concerned.)

Standing Order Service, Macmillan Distribution Ltd,
Houndmills, Basingstoke, Hampshire, RG21 2XS, England.

GROWTH AND STRUCTURAL CHANGE

Mark Cook and Nigel M. Healey

MACMILLAN

First published 1995 by
MACMILLAN PRESS LTD
Houndmills, Basingstoke, Hampshire RG21 2XS
and London
Companies and representatives
throughout the world

ISBN 0–333–56969–5

A catalogue record for this book
is available from the British Library.

10   9   8   7   6   5   4   3   2   1
04   03   02   01   00   99   98   97   96   95

Printed in Malaysia

Contents

List of Tables and Figures

Tables

Britain's Economic Growth Record

1

Over the decades countries in general and the UK in particular have become concerned about their relative growth rates. From a UK perspective the problem has been one of explaining why the UK growth rate has lagged behind its major competitors. Growth is seen as bringing many of the benefits required by society, in the form of improvements in real incomes and the ability to provide goods and services, to all sectors of the economy without having to resort to high levels of taxation in order that redistributions of income take place. The generation of growth may follow from a highly motivated, highly skilled and highly productive workforce, coupled with innovation, quality capital investment, and a high level of skill training and education. Thus the UK's slower growth rate has been blamed on the lack of these factors being in place, the result of which has led to the UK experiencing a decline in its percentage of total world manufactures. This chapter, therefore, concentrates on the major factors which have been put forward to explain the UK's poor growth record and in particular it highlights the performance of the UK economy over the 1980s. In this time period two contrasting points of view can be taken, firstly, that the Thatcher Administration has shaken British industry out of its lethargy and produced a manufacturing sector which is 'leaner and fitter'. In contrast there is the view that the 1980s have been no more successful than the late 1960s and early 1970s and that the cumulative effect of Conservative policies has been to alter UK industry only marginally; in other words, the 'Thatcher miracle' has been overstated.

Economic Growth Defined

Economic growth may be defined as an increase in a country's productive
capacity, identifiable by a sustained and continuous rise in real national
income over a period of years. While economic growth could refer to
many different characteristics of an economy, the conventional definition
focuses on the capability of the economy to meet the desires of its population for goods and services. The most commonly used measure of the
economy's capacity to fulfil material desires is the nation's gross national
product (GNP), with changes in economic growth being expressed in
terms of GNP per capita.

It is important to distinguish between actual and potential economic
growth. The former is the percentage increase in national output: the
growth of what is actually produced measured in terms of a nation's Gross
National Product (GNP). Potential growth, however, is the speed at which
the economy could grow if it were to use all its resources. That is, none of
the nation's resources are left idle. Thus potential economic growth can be
increased if there is an improvement in the level of resources or if there is
an increase in the efficiency with which these resources are used, through
improvements in technology, by more efficient organisations or via
improved labour skills. Whether actual output increases will depend on
whether this increase in potential growth is exploited.

The distinction between actual and potential growth can be seen with
the use of a production possibility diagram (see Figure 1.1). The production possibility curve indicates the possible combinations of two goods
that can be produced at any one time. In the figure they are shown as good
X and good Y and the boundary, therefore, shows the potential output that
can be produced by an economy. Potential growth is illustrated by a shift
outward to the right of the curve, from I to II.

Even if the economy itself is not using its current resources efficiently,
it is possible in the short run that actual growth can arise by taking up
slack in the economy, and thereby using labour and machinery to their full
capacities. For actual growth to be sustained over a number of years,
however, there would have to be an increase in potential output, that is the
production possibility curve would have to shift to the right. The idea of
the production possibility curve can also be used to illustrate the distinction or choice an economy makes between capital goods and consumption
goods.

Economic growth can be accelerated if resources are used to focus on
longrun consumption activities, that is, capital goods. Such an economy is
using its resources in a way that expands the output from its use of current
resources. In doing so, an economy incurs an opportunity cost of the

current consumption goods forgone. Thus we can adapt our production possibility curve, Figure 1.1, to show the trade-off between capital good production and consumption good production.

FIGURE 1.1
Production Possibilities and Growth

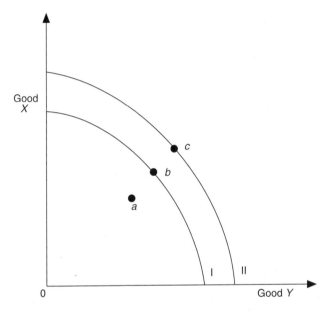

If we choose point *A* rather than point *B* we are trading off consumption goods for capital goods, forgoing consumption goods now so that in the future we can have more of both capital goods and consumption goods. Once again economic growth can be seen by an outward shift of the production possibility frontier (see Figure 1.2).

Since resources are the elements used to create goods and services, increases in their number and improvements in their quality stimulates economic growth. When the population grows or the numbers entering the labour market increase, there are more labour resources available for production purposes. But it is not only the number of workers available but also the quality of this labour force that must be considered. Techniques that promise to expand the knowledge, energy, achievement, motivation and creativity of potential employees are sources of future economic growth. In fact, if we improve the quality of human resources we can expand productive potential without needing an increase in the labour force.

FIGURE 1.2
Productive Possibilities Curve

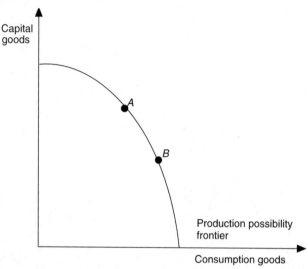

Capital goods are also essential for economic growth. An increasing labour force that uses out-of-date or inefficient machinery will soon experience declining output per person, given the law of diminishing returns. The quality and quantity of capital may increase through additional investment, improvements in technology, the willingness of a capital market to loan funds over the long term, through research and development (R&D), and through the willingness of entrepreneurs to invest in their home economy rather than invest abroad.

Britain's Economic Record

Table 1.1 indicates the British economy's growth record relative to other countries as well as illustrating a suitable comparison of the postwar years with earlier eras. The figures are based on national accounts statistics with output measured in constant prices. Although the table describes trends in labour productivity it also indicates a fairly accurate measure or compari-

TABLE 1.1
Growth Rates of Real Output per Worker Employed (% per annum)

	UK	USA	France	Germany	Japan
1873–99	1.2	1.9	1.3	1.5	1.1
1899–1913	0.5	1.3	1.6	1.5	1.8
1913–24	0.3	1.7	0.8	–0.9	3.2
1924–37	1.0	1.4	1.4	3.0	2.7
1937–51	1.0	2.3	1.7	1.0	–1.3
1951–64	2.3	2.5	4.3	5.1	7.6
1964–73	2.6	1.6	4.6	4.4	8.4
1973–79	1.2	–0.2	2.8	2.9	2.9
1979–87	2.1	0.6	1.8	1.5	2.9

SOURCES   Matthews, R.C.O., Feinstein, C.H. and Odling-Smee, J. (1982), *British Economic Growth, 1865–1973*, Stanford University Press, p. 31; and Organisation for Economic Co-operation and Development (OECD) (1988) *Historical Statistics, 1960–1987*, OECD, Paris.

son of the growth in real income per person which has tended to follow a similar pattern. Table 1.1 denotes, therefore, the long-standing peacetime tendency for the the UK to show a slower growth in labour productivity than our major competitors. Moreover, the table reveals that there has been a general slow-down in productivity growth after 1973, a fall that has lasted too long to be readily explained by short-term demand shocks, and it further indicates that after 1979 there was a relative improvement of the UK in the growth league, although in absolute terms productivity growth did not regain the level of the 1960s.

Up to 1979, although income per head grew in the UK, in other major developed nations it grew at a faster rate. This time-period also saw a large reduction in the UK's share of world manufactures, something that some would define as a process of deindustrialisation (see Chapter 3). Measured in terms of US dollars at 1970 prices the UK advanced from a per capita GDP of 2094 in 1950 to 3981 in 1979, whereas Germany moved from 1374 to 4946 and Japan from 585 to 4419. In terms of the share of world manufactured exports, the UK had a share of 25.4 per cent in 1950 though this had fallen to 11.2 per cent in 1969 and to 9 per cent in 1991. In employment terms those involved with manufacturing in the UK were reduced from 8.2 million (36.9 per cent of total employment) in 1969 to 7.2 million (32.1 per cent) in 1979 and 4.2 million (20.1 per cent) in 1993.

What of specific industry sectors? Although employment in manufacturing has declined since the Second World War and the UK's percentage of world trade declined, it does not mean that the UK's output of manufactured goods has declined, nor can we say that UK productivity has declined.

Table 1.2 indicates the changes in manufacturing productivity levels in the UK and other major OECD countries over the decades since 1975. It indicates that until the 1980s there was a persistent tendency for other OECD countries to have higher productivity growth rates than the UK, especially Germany and Japan. It is acknowledged that post-war reconstruction aided Germany's and Japan's productivity growth during the 1950s but after this period, and especially from 1959 onwards, German productivity rates outstripped those in the UK, giving the Germans a 60 per cent lead by the end of the 1970s. The improved productivity record of the UK during the 1980s appears to have reduced the German lead and their superiority in manufacturing productivity has now been reduced to the level seen during the mid-1970s. Even so, by the end of the 1980s German manufacturing productivity levels were over 29 per cent higher than in Britain and there does not appear to be any further narrowing of the productivity gap.

To summarise at this stage, a major productivity gap emerged between the US and the UK before the Second World War which has subsequently not been bridged. In addition, the productivity lead the UK had over its European neighbours had been lost by the late 1960s. The major weak-

TABLE 1.2
Manufacturing Productivity Growth: Annual per cent Change in Real Value Added per Person Employed

	1975–80	1980–85	1985–90
United Kingdom	0.9	5.4	4.0
Japan	7.3	6.0	3.9
United States	1.7	4.4	3.6
Italy	5.7	1.8	3.3
France	4.0	2.1	3.2
Germany	3.6	2.6	2.0
Average	3.8	3.8	3.3

SOURCE   Institute of Electrical Engineers (1992) *UK Manufacturing*, May.

nesses appear also to be in manufacturing rather than in services. Although some of this relative decline has been reversed, in comparison with the Japanese manufactures there has been no reversal in the productivity gap. Of course, the UK position in any productivity league depends upon the years in which we wish to judge the UK economy. The Treasury in 1989 described the UK economy of the 1980s as growing faster than any other major industrial economy. However, the period in question begins in a slump and ends at the top of a boom; therefore, the Treasury figures measure expansion during the recovery phase of the cycle, but not over the whole cycle. If a revised calculation is made, starting from the previous peak in 1979, we find that the rates of growth claimed by the Treasury are reduced quite dramatically: from 2.8 to 2.2 per cent per annum for GDP, and from 2.6 to 2.1 per cent per annum for GDP per worker. For the manufacturing sector the corresponding average annual peak-to-peak growth rates are 0.9 per cent for output, and 4.2 per cent for productivity.

If we take the whole economy, rather than just concentrating on manufacturing, and adjust for hours worked, the same trends still persist; that is, the UK economy lags behind its major competitors, though this time the results are not so marked (see Table 1.3). Of interest here is the much

TABLE 1.3
Real GDP per Hour Worked: Comparisons with the UK in Selected Years

	UK	*USA*	*France*	*Germany*	*Japan*
1870	100	97	48	50	17
1890	100	113	49	55	19
1913	100	135	60	65	23
1929	100	158	70	65	30
1938	100	154	82	73	35
1950	100	185	70	54	24
1960	100	188	84	84	33
1973	100	156	105	100	62
1979	100	150	114	113	70
1986	100	133	119	105	68

SOURCES   Feinstein, C.H., (1988) 'Economic Growth since 1870: Britain's Performance in International Perspective', *Oxford Review of Economic Policy*, vol. 14, no. 1, p. 4; amended in accordance with Maddison, A. (1989) *The World Economy in the Twentieth Century*, Paris, OECD.

superior performance of the US economy in the years 1870 to 1950, and the poor performance of the Japanese economy if we include the relatively poor performance of other sectors along with manufacturing.

Therefore, we need to address ourselves to the following questions:

1. Why has the UK had a much slower growth rate than many of its major competitors until recently?
2. Can the subsequent improved performance of the UK economy during the 1980s be related to policies conducted by the various Conservative Administrations and in particular the 'Thatcher legacy'?

Explanations of Britain's Growth Record

One approach to the explanations of economic growth is to analyse growth by the contributions made by the various inputs in the productive process, such as capital, labour and total factor productivity (TFP). It is now possible to measure the growth attributed to factor productivity if we have estimates for the contribution to growth from capital and labour (see Table 1.4).

Allowing for the fact that labour and capital have changed in quality over time, so that TFP growth will reflect improvements in technology and the more efficient use of resources, Table 1.4 indicates that the period between 1960 and 1973 represents a particularly high TFP growth for both the UK and other countries. Since 1974 TFP growth has slowed markedly in most countries though relatively less in Britain. Between 1960 and 1973 Britain experienced much slower growth than Germany, France and Japan. Compared with these countries, slower TFP growth accounted for 52, 75 and 29 per cent respectively of the gap in growth rates, and capital accumulation was responsible for 31, 7 and 31 per cent respectively. The results are to some extent not surprising since the postwar period was one in which there was a massive amount of reconstruction occurring in Europe and this was coupled with the diversion of resources out of agriculture and into the manufacturing sector.

If the growth accounting equation is to be believed, then growth of capital per worker (via investment) and of output per unit of total input (via improved efficiency and technological progress) are related directly to growth of real output per worker and we should concern ourselves with these when we are discussing the UK's growth record.

To some extent the poor performance of the UK economy could be due to general worldwide problems, such as the 1991–3 recession, and we

TABLE 1.4
Productivity in the Business Sector (Percentage Changes at Annual Rates)

	Total Factor Productivity			Labour Productivity			Capital Productivity		
	1960–73	1974–79	1980–91	1960–73	1974–79	1980–91	1960–73	1974–79	1980–91
United States	1.6	0.2	0.5	2.2	0.5	1.0	0.1	-0.5	-0
Japan	5.5	2.1	1.9	8.3	3.6	2.9	-2.8	-2.2	-1
Germany	2.6	2.2	1.2	4.5	3.4	1.8	-1.4	-0.4	-0
France	3.9	1.8	1.5	5.4	3.1	2.4	0.9	-0.9	-0
Italy	4.4	1.9	1.1	6.3	2.7	1.8	0.4	0.2	-0
United Kingdom	2.3	1.3	1.6	3.6	2.3	2.2	-0.6	-0.9	0

SOURCE Organisation for Economic Co-operation and Development (1993) *World Economic Outlook*, Paris, OECD.

shall need to distinguish between these types of wider factors and poor growth due to domestic circumstances. We may also want to consider a sectorial approach, for example growth in the manufacturing sector, or whether the poor growth record is one which pervades all sectors of the economy. Finally, the concern with the UK's poor growth record after the Second World War was not a new phenomenon; economists had sought to find explanations to the decline in the UK between the wars. It does not follow, however, that the reasons for the slower growth after the Second World War are the same as those put forward to explain the problems between the wars.

The following factors are some of the most prominent hypotheses put forward to explain the poor economic performance of the UK economy.

Fiscal Policy

One suggestion was that the various attempts by governments to stabilise the growth in the economy led to a variety of 'stop–go' policies which rather than stabilise growth had destabilised it. Without a consistent range of policies, the uncertainties that have ensued have resulted in a relatively poor investment record. More importantly it could be argued that the role of short-termism had been detrimental to the UK economy compared with other countries which had advocated longer-term goals.

The Bacon and Eltis argument was somewhat different. (See R. Bacon and W. Eltis, *Britain's Economic Problem: Too Few Producers*, 2nd edn (London: Macmillan, 1978).) They suggested that government expenditure had 'crowded out' private-sector investment thereby inhibiting the UK's growth potential. They distinguished two main sectors in the economy, the 'non-marketed sector' (public sector) and the 'marketed sector' (private sector). Any surplus of output over consumption in the marketed sector was potentially available for net exports, investment in the marketed sector or could be diverted for use in the non-marketed sector. In their view, since the beginning of the 1960s this surplus had increasingly been used for the third approach.

One method of obtaining this excess of output over consumption via the non-marketed sector is with the use of taxes; Bacon and Eltis suggested that workers, when faced with a rise in taxes on their income, simply requested and obtained pay rises commensurate with any rise in taxation. This increased the costs to industry and thereby reduced investment potential and so economic growth. In other words, wage rigidity was seen as an important factor inhibiting export growth.

The Balance of Payments Constraint

As an economy grows during the economic cycle it is possible that the higher level of economic activity serves to drag in imports, and the growth process is constrained through the need to achieve a balance on the external account. It has been argued that the elasticities facing the UK in terms of its trade are less favourable than those faced by other countries. In this case, when the economy grows the UK runs into balance of payments difficulties which could be resolved if the real exchange rate were free to vary. Thus when the UK economy grows it 'sucks in' imports not only of raw materials and semi-manufactured goods but also of finished commodities. Allowing the exchange rate to depreciate would restore balance in the trade account. The chief obstacle to this process is that increased import prices feed through to inflation and trade unions may be expected to resist any reduction in their real incomes. Thus the depreciation in the currency is usually offset by an increase in money wages.

Productivity Growth and the Structure of Employment

By using the following equation, known as Verdoorn's Law,

$$pm = \alpha + bem$$

where *pm* is the rate of growth of output per worker, *em* is the rate of growth of employment and *b*>0, output growth encourages productivity growth in manufacturing which could be related to dynamic economies of scale. Given that the UK was the first country to industrialise and that its agricultural labour force was small, then this, it is argued, exhausted the economy's ability to expand manufacturing employment and reduced the UK's growth potential relative to other countries. Secondly, the development of North Sea oil pushed up the UK's exchange rate, making imports more price competitive and exports less competitive and by doing so had reduced productivity growth. Moreover, there appeared to be a 'vicious circle' involved here from which the UK could not escape; that is, balance of payments constraints slow down the growth in the economy which thereby retards productivity growth which causes the UK to become less competitive and this leads to a further balance of payments problem.

Supply-side Problems

The area of supply-side factors will be detailed in Chapter 6, none the less the various factors which have been suggested as inhibiting the market mechanism will be outlined here. Amongst the factors which have been put forward as explanations of the UK's poor productivity record are: ob-structive industrial relations and trade union restrictive practices; unskilled and inadequately trained workers and management; poorly directed R&D, and distortions that arise due to the tax system. In addition there has been a tendency for British management to look towards short-term profits for their shareholders rather than to look for long-term investment potential. Some even argue that the 'climate' in the UK is not one for taking up new ideas, and thus other countries reap the long-term benefit from these. In addition, the financing of UK industry through capital markets in the UK rather than through the *Kieretsu* organisation in Japan or through the *Hausbank* process in Germany has resulted in a lack of finance on some occasions and less consistent policies on the other.

These factors, therefore, indicate widespread market failure to achieve the most efficient use of economic resources. This suggests that some form of government intervention might be required to make the market work more efficiently, though critics of this approach simply see it as exacer-bating the problem. It has also been pointed out that the role of special-in-terest groups in stable democracies have tended to retard the resource allocations necessary for full exploitation of improved technological poss-ibilities. Unless disrupted by external factors such as war, this leads to what has been termed the 'sclerosis' problem. The UK is a prime example.

With a background of poor relative growth due to a combination of the factors outlined above, to what extent did the Thatcher Decade restore Britain's position in world growth?

The Thatcher Miracle?

It would appear that during the 1980s UK productivity growth improved relative to the rest of the European Union, though not relative to the remainder of the OECD. Moreover there are those who believe that the pieces are now in place for further productivity gains in the future.

Table 1.5 indicates a number of important features. First, the US which is the highest technology economy has always grown slower than other countries(the technology frontier argument), and secondly, other countries have had much higher growth rates than the US since they have been in the 'catch-up' phase. But where does this leave the UK? The UK during

TABLE 1.5
Performance Indicators

	Output per Worker (% pa)			
	1966–73	*1973–79*	*1979–83*	*1983–88*
United Kingdom	3.2	1.3	2.1	1.7
EC (9)	4.2	2.2	1.2	1.8
OECD other	3.0	1.1	1.3	2.1
US	1.2	0.0	0.2	1.3
Japan	7.9	2.9	2.4	3.4
Sweden	2.8	0.5	0.9	1.8
OECD total	3.5	1.5	1.3	2.0

SOURCES   Organisation for Economic Co-operation and Development (1987) *Economic Outlook*, June, Paris, and earlier issues; together with OECD, *National Accounts, 1960–1985*, Paris.

the 1960s and 1970s fell appreciably behind the rest of Europe and because of this it might be expected that some relative improvement would have occurred in the 1980s. The figures suggest that something did appear to happen during the 1980s, since in the UK output per worker grew appreciably relative to most countries. So why has productivity grown so fast in the UK relative to continental Europe? It is unlikely to be due to capital stock growth or to relatively high R&D, since during the 1980s both tended to be lower in the UK than in other EC or OECD countries. It is also not due to the 'playing the best batsman argument' since the closure of manufacturing plants during the early 1980s included a number of larger plants with above-average productivity levels. Productivity growth could have occurred because production has been reorganised due to the curbing of trade union power and through reductions in manning levels. Some of the impetus for these changes has not been due to domestic policies alone but to a combination of domestic and external pressures. Such factors would include the world recession in 1980–1 exacerbated by the Conservative policies which gave workers and management an obvious choice; to change working practices and increase productivity or lose their jobs entirely. The massive external shock to the system of the world recession was further sustained during the 1980s by various pieces of labour market legislation and continued high unemployment which switched the balance of power in wage negotiations in favour of management. Thus productivity gains were readily available because people did not wish to lose their jobs. Given the demise of trade union power, it proved easier to introduce European and Japanese working practices which would generate these improvements in productivity. Layard and Nickell note, 'productivity growth has been higher in more unionised firms and also higher in those that sustained a bigger shock in 1979–81' (R. Layard and S.Nickell, 'Mrs Thatcher's Miracle?', *Economic Affairs* (Dec.–Jan. 1990) pp. 6–9). The main problem they see in the future is that the productivity gap between UK plants and similar European plants will become harder to close due to the fact that the level of training in the UK is inadequate and this will constrain productivity improvements.

Alternatively, productivity growth in the UK during the 1980s can be explained by the same factors that have affected productivity growth over the previous three decades, such as changes in energy prices, the rate of investment, and capital utilisation, rather than the efforts of the Thatcher government to reduce union power, to encourage entrepreneurial risk-taking, to remove declining industries and the like. The productivity growth rates of the 1980s are simply a return to the long-run trend experienced in the UK economy not a move to a higher trend. Of course, there can still be short-term fluctuations around this long-term trend, such as variations in the real exchange rate or changes in the real money stock, but if long-term productivity growth is to be obtained there is a need for an energy policy to shield domestic producers from external shocks, direct incentives to stimulate investment and methods by which the transfer of technology can take place from one country to another and for this to be willingly absorbed into mainstream productive capacities. In this last area the problems with the level of education and training for employees and employers, poor industrial relations, the influence of entrenched interest groups and the lack of long-term bank finance together with the short-termism of investment plans suggest that such a scenario may not be forthcoming in the UK's case.

The role of new technology and the microchip revolution is also relevant to the UK's 'productivity miracle'. However, such technology is also available to our major competitors and so by itself it cannot be a complete explanation of the UK's improved competitiveness. But it is possible that UK industry is making better use of new technologies now due perhaps to union flexibility and government incentives to industry. By increasing employment it is possible that workers are more flexible in the job market and that the balance of power has switched towards management rather than being with the 'shop floor'. Moreover we should not forget the way in which companies are run. The 1980s have seen a big reduction in overmanning and this in itself has improved productivity.

Although the Thatcher Administrations have brought to bear some important supply-side measures on the UK economy, in terms of the manufacturing sector some argue that the long-standing sources of structural weakness in production have not been tackled. Recent productivity gains have not stemmed from a fundamental reorganisation of the forces of production in Britain, but instead are the product of a series of step-by-step changes dictated by short-term rather than long-term aims and perspectives. Such a view is not held by all, since others suggest that manufacturing has recovered sufficiently to take the place of oil when it enters its declining phase, and that manufacturing is sufficiently well placed for sustainable productivity growth in the future.

In Nolan's view the productivity changes in the UK economy are the product of three basic ingredients: 'the recovery of output since 1982, accompanied by continuing largescale job losses; a power shift in the relationship between employer and employee; and changes in work organisation and production technology' (P. Nolan, 'Walking on Water?: Performance and Industrial Relations under Thatcher', *Industrial Relations Journal*, vol. 20, no. 2, 1989). It is the interaction of these three that has resulted in a series of step-by-step increases in measured productivity rather than any fundamental change in production relations. In other words, the Thatcher legacy has altered the veneer rather than the substance of the problem. Moreover, Nolan points to the fact the the UK has at the same time seen a dramatic structural change in its industrial base towards low-skill, low-technology production which means it is subject to much more competition from the Newly Industrialised Countries (NICs). In addition, there have been no major changes in the modernisation of production conditions – low levels of investment have been one of the main areas in which the UK has been criticised – but that there has been a series of inch-by-inch changes which have often been geared towards labour intensification. It would appear, therefore, that the effect of the Thatcher Administrations on Britain's overall performance is open to question.

Moreover, by targeting inflation as the number one priority, employment has been sacrificed and this higher natural rate of unemployment may in itself have enabled more flexible arrangements in the labour market. None the less, the supply-side measures introduced by the Conservatives appear to have pushed the UK back towards its long-term growth trend. Increased international capital mobility and lower inflation coincided with more and better-quality investment. The danger is that without sufficient training the growth in productivity may fall back once again.

Within the context of the 1980s there appears to be no single answer to why the UK economy has 'turned around'. The UK's problems appear to relate to a number of factors which would include poor-quality management, the inheritance of a 'poor' industrial structure, unhelpful industrial relations, relatively weak R&D by the industrial sector, and inadequate training. There is little conclusive evidence as to which of these is more important than the others. Evidence as to whether the 1980s saw a break-through for UK industry in those problem areas outlined above is patchy. The 1980s did see a rise in the UK's relative position in the growth league, even though this was aided by the exhaustion of the 'catch-up' in other countries. Part of this can be explained by unions who were willing to accept new conditions and working practices given the rise in unemployment; firms also reduced overmanning as competitive conditions worsened for them. Such features did not appear to happen in countries such as Germany and France whose industrial structures were different. In the public sector there were also marked improvements as unions were defeated, and privatisation got under way. The increase in competition could also be felt by firms as the government reduced subsidies to industry, import penetration grew and world tariffs were reduced.

The role of income tax within this reform programme is difficult to judge and there is little conclusive evidence to suggest that its reduction made workers more productive. None the less, the UK still appeared to perform less well in R&D during the 1980s. Part of the blame is put on the cost of capital in the UK, the role of short-termism and the fact that UK firms are more prone to takeovers which may reduce their long-term commitment to R&D. Education and training, however, still appears to be a weakness of the UK economy. It may well be that the shake-out that has occurred in UK industry is a 'one-off' and the 1990s will see a return to more sober levels of growth.

The UK – the First Post-industrial Nation?

Whichever way we look at it, the UK's growth performance was poor relative to its major industrial competitors during the 1960s and 1970s. This was no new phenomenon in relation to the US, but more disturbing was the way that the UK was overhauled in the growth league by the Japanese and other major European industrial countries. Currently, the UK is lying around seventeenth in the world in terms of GNP per head.

There may well be some major underlying problems that the UK economy faces outside the political sphere, and one suggestion is that because the UK was the first industrialised nation it will become the first post-industrialised nation. None the less, there is the view that the UK economy suffers from structural weaknesses and that the 'Thatcher revolution' was a means by which some of the frictions in various markets could be overcome. The measure of success of these policies, some would say, is seen with the improvement of the UK's productivity level during the 1980s and the increase in its share of total world manufactures during the 1990s. Others would say that the policies adopted in the 1980s have given a 'one-off' effect and that the improvement in the UK economy is not sustainable. Furthermore, at what cost were these improvements obtained? Perhaps, however, the UK economy will never truly catch up, since a future single currency and the single European market may encourage convergence in variables in which the UK needs a comparative advantage. Moreover, could it be that we are structurally different to other countries and that to try and emulate these other countries is not possible? It is to this question that we now turn in Chapter 2.

Growth and Structural Change in the British Economy

2

Like many other developed economies over the last 30 years the UK's industrial structure has altered from a predominantly manufacturing economy towards a more service-orientated one. Unlike other developed nations, however, which possessed relatively high levels of agricultural employment the UK compensated for the growth in service sector employment by a reduction in manufacturing employment. This feature of the changes in the relative sectors of labour employment in the 'maturing economy' is perhaps too simplistic an explanation of the structural changes in the UK economy, since it does not make clear why the UK, rather than Germany or Japan, experienced a decline in its share of world manufacturing output. Within the UK there may be factors which are singularly British, such as the role of North Sea oil and the impact of the non-marketed sector in crowding out private sector investment, which may be relevant in explaining the structural change. It may well be that the structural changes in the UK have been brought about by concentrating on products for which it possessed a comparative advantage, that is services, or that the UK was 'unfortunate' in possessing a poor industrial structure. Let us examine these factors in more detail.

An Overview of Structural Change

Structural change is often referred to in terms of changes in the three main sectors of an economy: the primary, secondary and tertiary sectors. The primary sector includes all activities related to the extraction of natural resources, such as farming and mining. The secondary sector includes activities related to the production of goods and the processing of materials. Manufacturing is the main constituent of this sector though it also includes the construction sector and the utility industries such as gas, electricity and water. Finally, we have the tertiary sector which includes both private and public sector services such as insurance and banking and health and defence.

By structural change we mean variations in the relative size of these sectors which can be seen in terms of changes in output, employment and productivity. In fact the term 'restructuring' involves not only the changing composition of industries or of the labour force but more generally changes in the terms and relations under which the process of capital accumulation for profit takes place.

Restructuring of the economy may take place suddenly, in response to an external or political factor for example, or the change can take place gradually. In the case of the former, economists of the Austrian School tend to see market adjustments as periodic radical realignments of values necessitating sharp policy changes. These sharp policy changes can be in many directions, one of which, it could be argued, was 'Thatcherism'.

On the other hand, we would expect the structure of an economy to change slowly over time as the pattern of demand changes, as a result of increases in income and changes in tastes. Thus these alterations will have knock-on effects on employment and output. One such example of this would be to look at products whose income elasticities of demand are high, such as cars, white goods and electronic goods, demand for which has increased over time compared with food and other basic necessities whose income elasticities of demand are low. An economy which produces a relatively high proportion of low income elasticity products may well run into balance of payments problems, through low growth and low productivity, if it does not change the composition of its output. The pattern of demand is also responsive to changes in the age distribution of the population. The general feature of the UK, like most other developed nations, is for its population pyramid to be mushroomed-shaped, that is, with a growing proportion of older people in the population. Different age groups may well have different tastes and therefore, over time, we should see a movement towards producing products for this older age group. Market forces will encourage this as the older age groups have an increasingly important role to play with their purchasing power. Likewise in terms of products we should see reduced demand for education, housing and so on, but increased demand for leisure facilities and medical care.

The supply side also has a role to play in any structural changes. The decline in the younger cohorts who are entering the labour market has resulted in increased income relative to other sectors of employment, encouraging some sectors to take on older workers or encouraging workers to return to the labour market. An example is B&Q, the DIY chain, which had a policy of employing mature workers during the economic boom of the 1980s when it became difficult to obtain workers from younger age groups. The impact of technology has also altered the pattern of goods and services that can be provided from the market as technical progress has reduced the cost of production. In doing so some workers have been displaced, though at the same time the impact of technology has increased employment in those sectors or goods for which a country previously did not possess a comparative advantage.

The impact of oil on the economy has also been of great importance in the structural changes in the UK. The rise in the price of oil during the 1970s served to encourage developed economies who were major oil importers to seek substitute sources of energy. This helped to encourage the development of North Sea oil, and brought to the fore the need to be energy-efficient in production processes. The world recession which followed also had important consequences for energy-intensive sectors such as steel, thereby causing changes in secondary sector output. Conversely, the development of North Sea oil had very different effects on the UK economy. It is argued that UK manufacturers did not have to 'try so hard' to keep the balance of payments under control since the oil sector did just that.

The development of oil also had important consequences for the UK exchange rate. The huge surplus on the oil account and the subsequent surplus in the balance of payments (see Chapter 4 and elsewhere in this chapter) served to make the pound a petro-currency. This meant that the value of sterling was much more subject to changes in the price of oil and in the early 1980s kept sterling's value much higher than it otherwise would have been. The rise in the value of the pound during the early 1980s made UK exports less competitive and imports more competitive, leading to one of the factors which caused the process of deindustrialisation, discussed in Chapter 3. This process of deindustrialisation has been seen in the decline in the manufacturing sector, reducing output in the early 1980s to levels below that of the early 1970s and reducing employment in this sector.

On the international stage the growth of international competition can also be viewed as one of the forces behind the change in the structure of the UK economy. The greater productivity of many of the UK's trading partners has resulted in many of Britain's traditional industries losing market share over the past three decades, through a process of lower productivity, lower investment, less R&D, poor management, restrictive practices by unions, pay deals not linked to productivity, and the consequences of inflation. For most products the major impact on UK output and employment has come from the major trading nations within Europe rather than from Japan and the rest of the world. The entry of the UK into the EC in 1973 has also had profound effects on the market access offered to many mainland European firms. Moreover, the UK has had to accept a pattern of trade which mirrors the comparative advantages of EC trade.

Structural Change in the UK

Changes in Output

Table 2.1 shows index numbers of output at constant factor cost for the three main sectors of the UK economy. As we can see, for the primary sector, agriculture, forestry and fishing grew slowly to the late 1970s but more rapidly thereafter as a result of EC policies. The concern about the problems of over-production and food surpluses and the problems of over-fishing have resulted in this sector reducing output by the end of the decade. The decline of the coal and coke industry is self-evident, partly due to cheaper coal imports, the Conservative administrations' privatisation policy which led to the electricity and gas companies reviewing their arrangements with the coal industry, the desire to make the coal industry profitable by reducing the number of inefficient pits, the decline in manufacturing, and the greater efficiency in the use of energy. Conversely, there has been a rapid rise in the output from oil and natural gas, which rose sharply after North Sea oil began to come on stream in the late 1970s. Growth thereafter averaged 6.4 per cent per annum until 1986. Since this period there has been a downturn in output from the North Sea, primarily because the price of energy has decreased and also because the UK has passed the peak of production from its North Sea fields (see also Chapter 4 for the contribution of North Sea oil to the balance of payments).

For the secondary sector 1973 was a peak year for output in both manu-facturing and construction. From then on, output from these two sectors actually fell fairly slowly until 1979 and more rapidly thereafter. Not until 1988 did the output from these two sectors reach the previous peak of 1973. Since then output has grown more slowly in these two sectors and actually fell back during the UK recession of 1991–3.

The index of the production industries shows an upward trend apart from the 1979–81 period. The production industries include manu-facturing as well as oil and gas production, therefore some of the

TABLE 2.1
Index Numbers of Output at Constant Factor Cost (1980 = 100)

	1964	1969	1973	1979	1981	1986	1988	1990	1991
Primary									
Agriculture, forestry and fishing	69.3	73.5	87.4	90.1	102.6	118.8	117.8	126.3	129.6
Coal and coke	205	148.8	114	97.6	97.3	79.3	78.4	69.4	69.1
Extraction of mineral oil and natural gas	—	0.3	2.2	98.7	110.3	153.0	136.1	110.9	113.4
Secondary									
Mineral oil processing	75.3	99.9	126.9	113.7	93.0	99.0	107.4	109.1	113.1
Manufacturing	87.6	103.0	114.1	109.5	94.0	104.7	117.9	122.2	116.0
Construction	104.2	117.6	122.4	105.8	89.9	102.1	128.1	137.4	120.2
Other energy and water supply	56.7	68.9	87.1	102.2	99.6	112.2	120.3	122.6	127.0
Tertiary									
Distribution, hotels, catering, repairs	85.8	92.2	107	107.9	98.4	120.4	136	141.4	135.0
Transport	76.5	84.8	100.8	103.6	99.0	108.7	123.7	130.5	126.2
Communication	49.8	65.5	81.8	97.2	102.2	130.8	145.6	163.1	162.1
Banking, finance, insurance, business services and leasing	53	66	81	95	104	154	185.8	201.2	191.5
Ownership of dwellings	69	80	87	99	101	107	108.3	110.4	111.3
Public administration, national defence and compulsory social security	86	90	99	99	101	99	101	103.0	100.0
Education and health services	62	72	82	99	101	105	112.6	113.6	112.3
Other services	72	76	82	95	98	120	134	139.6	133.7
GDP	75.6	85.5	96.4	103	98.4	114	125	128.7	125.0
Production industries	76.6	89.7	99.5	107.1	96.6	110.2	118.1	117.8	114.2

SOURCE   Central Statistical Office, *National Income and Expenditure* 'Blue Book', various editions: 1983 table 2.3; 1987b, table 1.5 and table 2.4, 1990 table 2.4, 1992 table 2.4 (rebased from 1985 to 1980), CSO, London.

downturn in manufacturing output is disguised by a rise in oil and gas production. After 1981, the growth of UK industrial output resumed its upward trend assisted by the recovery of manufacturing output. During the 1960s and 1970s industrial production in the UK lagged behind its major trading partners, though by the early 1980s the UK had a superior performance. For example, between 1981 and 1987 industrial production in the UK grew at 16.5 per cent whilst for the OECD as a whole the growth rate was 14 per cent. However, if we move on to the end of the decade and take a slightly different time period, from 1985 to 1990, UK industrial production rose only 10.3 per cent whilst the OECD average was 15.2 per cent. In other words, depending on which years we wish to take we can argue that either the UK out-performed the rest of its major trading partners or that its performance was, as it has often been, behind that of the other major trading nations. If the latter is to be believed then the early 1980s period of 'catch-up' by the UK economy is now over.

In the tertiary sector output has grown for all areas even during the 1979–81 recession, apart for distribution, hotels, catering and transport. Of major interest is the growth in banking, insurance and financial services as well as those for communications. At the same time we can see that public sector services took a smaller and smaller share of total output (see Table 2.2). The growth in the service sector between 1965 and 1980 was smaller in the UK than for the OECD countries. This can partly be explained by the comparative advantage that the UK had experienced in this sector and its high level of development, compared with other countries 'catching-up' from a much lower level. During the 1980s the performance of the UK service sector matched that of the other OECD countries. One of the constraints on the UK's service sector during this period can be attributed to the fact that many services are linked to industry; thus if the manufacturing base was being eroded at this time then there was less demand for services.

Changes in the Shares of Output

Over the period 1964–90 the primary sector was in decline as a proportion of total output in the UK. For agriculture this is not just a UK phenomenon, for in the EC the share of agriculture in the Community's GDP was halved between 1960 and 1980; this was due to both the relative contraction of agriculture and the expansion of other sectors of the economy. In addition the utilised agricultural area has also been contracting in most member states. The figures once again hide important changes in the overall composition of the sector since oil and gas production have contributed greatly to the primary sector's position. In 1984, for example, the

TABLE 2.2
Percentage Shares of GDP at Factor Cost*

	1964	1969	1973	1979	1986	1988	1990	1991
Primary	5.8	4.3	4.2	6.7	5.3	3.8	3.3	3.7
Agriculture, forestry and fishing	1.9	1.8	2.9	2.2	1.7	1.3	1.4	1.7
Coal and coke	3.9	2.5	1.1	1.3	1.0	0.7	0.5	0.6
Extraction of mineral oil and natural gas	—	—	—	3.2	2.6	1.8	1.4	1.4
Secondary	40.8	42.0	40.9	36.7	32.2	31.3	31.3	29.8
Mineral oil processing	0.5	0.5	0.4	0.6	0.7	0.3	0.4	0.4
Manufacturing	29.5	30.7	30.0	27.3	23.0	22.4	21.2	19.9
Construction	8.4	8.4	7.3	6.2	5.8	6.2	7.2	6.4
Other energy and water supply	2.4	2.4	2.8	2.6	2.7	2.4	2.5	3.1
Tertiary	53.8	53.0	54.9	56.5	62.3	64.8	65.4	66.4
Distribution, hotels, catering, repairs	14.0	13.3	13.1	12.7	13.3	13.2	13.9	13.9
Transport	4.4	4.4	4.7	4.8	4.3	⎱ 6.9	6.7	6.6
Communication	1.6	1.9	2.3	2.5	2.6	⎰		
Banking, finance, insurance, business services and leasing	8.3	8.6	10.7	11.0	15.0	18.4	17.3	16.8
Ownership of dwellings	5.4	5.5	5.1	5.8	5.5	5.1	6.1	6.6
Public administration, national defence and compulsory social security	7.6	7.0	6.1	6.1	6.9	6.5	6.3	6.6
Education and health services	6.9	7.1	7.7	8.1	8.6	8.5	9.0	9.5
Other services	5.6	5.2	5.1	5.7	6.1	6.2	6.1	6.4

Calculated from GDP at factor cost, at current prices and unadjusted for financial services and residual error.

* Totals may not sum to 100 due to rounding.

SOURCE   Central Statistical Office, *National Income and Expenditure* 'Blue Book', various editions, 1983, 1985, 1987b, 1989, 1992, CSO, London.

contribution of the primary sector to total output was 9.5 per cent, most of which can be attributed to North Sea oil and gas production.

The secondary sector's share of output has also declined appreciably since 1964 to around 29 per cent by the beginning of the 1990s. This is due mainly to the decline of manufacturing's share of output, particularly after 1973. Although the decline slowed during the 1980s there has been no reversal in the long-run decline of the secondary sector's share of GDP.

The tertiary sector's share of GDP has grown throughout the period so that by 1991 over two-thirds of GDP was provided by this sector; in particular, we should notice the major growth in financial services.

The UK is not the only country to experience these types of changes in its industrial structure: most of the major industrial countries have seen similar trends. None the less, since the UK has grown at a slower rate than many of its major trading partners this means that its manufacturing sector has shrunk to a greater degree. To put this in perspective, it took manufacturing in the UK until 1987 to reach an output level which was equivalent to its previous peak in 1973.

Employment Levels

The numbers employed in each sector will be a reflection of the various output levels, the impact of technology, changes in working practices, changes in people's perceptions of each of the employment areas, and the state of the economy at the various times. In terms of the total employed in the primary sector the numbers were 70 per cent less in 1990 compared with 1964 and as a proportion of the workforce the primary sector provided 1.9 per cent in 1993. For the twelve European Community members, only 6.6 per cent of the total labour force was employed in the agricultural sector in 1991. The share of agriculture in total gross fixed capital formation remained stable at 4.0 per cent, suggesting a move towards higher capital intensity. The data also confirm that over a relatively long time period the agricultural sector of the Community has been experiencing a rapid increase in productivity, mostly because of the restructuring of the agricultural sector towards larger farms, of which the UK has the greatest number, and the fast pace of mechanisation and use of fertilizers (see Chapter 4 on the limits to growth). The funding mechanisms to support agriculture in the Community have also contributed to the rise in productivity of this sector. Despite this progress, the Community's relative productivity ratio between agriculture and the other sectors of the economy is still only 0.5. Finally, within the primary sector of the UK we can see the small proportion of workers involved with the extraction of oil and gas. In fact, the numbers employed in this sector have fallen over the 1980s and 1990s as the industry has reacted to lower oil prices.

In the secondary sector the main feature is the large fall in the number employed in manufacturing. From almost 9 million people employed in 1964 the numbers fell to around 4.1 million in 1993, resulting in a corresponding fall in manufacturing's share of total employment from 38.1 per cent to 20.1 per cent or a loss of 4.87 million jobs.

TABLE 2.3
World Trade Shares and Deindustrialisation (%)

(a) Shares of world trade in manufactures (%)

	1950	1960	1970	1979	1990	1991
France	9.9	9.6	8.7	10.5	9.7	10
Germany	7.3	19.3	19.8	20.9	20.2	20
Japan	3.4	6.9	11.7	13.7	15.9	17
UK	25.5	16.5	10.8	9.1	8.6	9
USA	27.3	21.6	18.6	16.0	16.0	18

SOURCES   Brown, C.J.F. and Sheriff, T.D. (1979) 'De-industrialisation: A Background Paper' in F. Blackaby (ed.), *De-industrialisation*, London, Heinemann; Central Statistical Office (1991) *Monthly Review of External Trade Statistics*, London, HMSO.

(b) Deployment of the labour force (%)

	France	Germany	Japan	UK	USA
1950					
Agriculture	27.4	23.2	41.0	4.9	11.9
Industry	37.0	44.4	24.2	49.4	35.9
Services	35.6	32.4	34.8	45.7	52.2
1970					
Agriculture	13.9	8.6	17.4	3.2	4.5
Industry	39.7	48.5	35.7	44.8	34.4
Services	46.4	42.9	46.9	52.0	61.1
1990					
Agriculture	6.1	3.4	7.2	2.1	2.8
Industry	30.0	39.7	34.1	28.8	26.2
Services	63.9	56.9	58.7	69.1	70.9

SOURCE   Crafts, N.F.R. (1992) 'Reversing Relative Economic Decline? The 1980s in Historical Perspective', *Oxford Review of Economic Policy*, vol. 7, no. 3, p. 85.

This fall in employment was partly compensated for by the rise in employment in the tertiary sector, particularly in financial services and the various scientific and professional services. Once again the restructuring of the economy towards a more service-orientated one is not a feature associated only with the UK. Table 2.3 shows the similar trend in France, Germany, Japan and the US.

However, whilst the growth in service sector employment in these countries has come from movements out of the agricultural sector, for the UK the movement is one from manufacturing to services.

Financial Services Sector

Table 2.4 indicates the relative shift of the two sectors of manufacturing and financial services in the UK. The reasons for the expansion of the financial services sector are manifold but include the fact that financial services may be viewed by the consumer as superior products which are positively related to income. As consumers become wealthier they are likely to seek more financial advice, and financial services can be seen both as an alternative to consumption and as an enhancement of it by bringing expenditure forward. Secondly, businesses and government require more financial services as the world becomes more sophisticated, perhaps even subcontracting out requests for services which used to be performed in-house. Some of the decline in manufacturing jobs may be due to this process of externalisation. Finally, one of the major goals of the Conservative Administration in 1979 was to liberalise financial services via the removal of exchange controls, the removal of the banking corset, reforming the Stock Exchange, and so on, and this led to further expansion of this sector.

If we examine the financial services sector more closely we see that it has enjoyed a fairly rapid growth in employment of around 5 per cent per year since 1979, though this has not affected all sectors equally. As Figure 2.1 shows, employment growth has been faster in business services, slightly slower in banking and at only around 2.5 per cent in insurance. In fact, in the early 1990s these last two sectors have been heavily involved in shedding jobs as profits have fallen. None the less, between 1979 and 1993 the number of jobs in the financial services sector increased from 1.6 million to 2.5 million. 'The majority of these jobs are to be found in London and the South East and the decreasing outward ripple effect towards the provinces is often focused on the major road corridors. Example of such developments would be the move of some major finance companies to Swindon and Nat West to Bristol'.

TABLE 2.4
The Shift in Employment in Great Britain (thousands)

	June 1979		June 1990		June 1993	
	Total	per cent of total emp.	Total	per cent of total emp.	Total	per cent of total emp.
Manufacturing industries	7,107	31.4	4,994	22.3	4,190	20.1
Total financial services	1,622	7.2	2,701	12.1	2,577	12.4
All industries and services	22,638		22,380		20,803	

SOURCE 'Employees in employment in Great Britain', *Employment Gazette*, table 1.2, January 1994, Department of Employment, London.

FIGURE 2.1
Employment Growth in Financial Services (% per year, 1979–90)

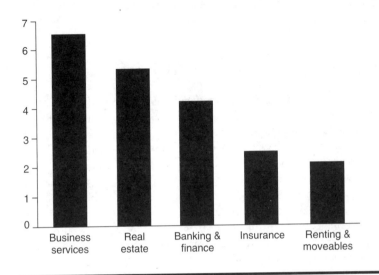

Source   *Lloyds Bank Economic Bulletin*, no. 145 (Jan. 1991) p. 1.

The future for this sector is not as bright as its past record suggests. There is not expected to be any major jobs boom; on the contrary, recession, bad debt provision and the impact of information technology are all likely to lead to a reduction in the number of jobs provided by this sector.

In terms of output, the financial services sector over the ten years to 1989 increased annually at a rate of growth of 7.3 per cent and, given the 5.1 per cent rise in employment, there has been a productivity increase of 2.2 per cent. This is slightly worse than productivity in the economy as a whole, but better than the other areas of the service sector.

On the other hand, the 7.3 per cent growth rate of financial services exceeded the 1.8 per cent average growth rate for the rest of the economy during the 1980s and in doing so raised the economy's overall growth rate to 2.3 per cent. It is estimated that if financial services had grown at the same rate as the economy as a whole then total GDP would have grown by 0.5 per cent a year less. Given that the growth rate in financial services is expected to slow down during the early 1990s then correspondingly this will impact on the overall level of growth of the economy. If this is the case, what other sector will emerge as the engine of growth for the UK economy?

Financial services is just one sub-sector that stands out in the structural change that has taken place in the UK economy. Within the context of economic growth and our subsequent discussion of deindustrialisation and the balance of payments one other sector deserves attention at this stage and that is, North Sea oil.

North Sea Oil and its Impact on the UK Economy

From being a net importer of oil in the early 1970s the UK became a net exporter of oil by the early 1980s, as Table 2.5 indicates. This build-up of oil production has raised a number questions as to the impact of oil on the UK economy, particularly in terms of structural change. One view is that the development of North Sea oil has led to the pound becoming a petro-currency with its value heavily dependent on the price of oil. Thus, the development of North Sea oil caused an appreciation of the pound and it was this fact that led to a deterioration in the size of the manufacturing sector. The plausibility of this analysis was easy to see in 1980 because sterling had risen to a record level in real terms and the manufacturing sector was declining rapidly. One estimate was that 20–25 per cent appreciation of the real exchange rate and a 15 per cent improvement in the terms of trade would be necessary to restore current account equilibrium after the development of oil. This would also be associated with a 6 per cent contraction in manufacturing output. There have been a number of criticisms of this perspective: first, because it failed to take account of the effects of rising oil prices during the 1970s; and, secondly, North Sea oil can only be a contributory factor since the process of deindustrialisation was well under way before the discovery of oil in the North Sea. But did North Sea oil harm the manufacturing sector through its impact on exchange rates? North Sea oil can enhance the manufacturing sector. Before it came on stream attempts to expand the economy confronted a balance of payments constraint. Oil, therefore, provided a significant saving of foreign exchange, thus easing the constraint on growth.

But what of the revenue from North Sea oil? The Bank of England noted that the UK was clearly better off with oil than in a scenario without oil; none the less, we are not that much better off than before the oil price hike of 1973–4. Is there, therefore, any concrete conclusion we can reach about the impact of oil on the economy? C. Bean, 'The Impact of North Sea Oil', in R. Dornbusch and R. Layard (eds), *The Performance of the UK Economy* (London: Oxford University Press, 1987) pp. 64–96) suggests that the question is virtually meaningless because it is incompletely specified:

TABLE 2.5
Components of the UK Current Account (£m)

Year	Total	Visible Balance Oil	Visible Balance Non-oil	Invisible Balance Total	Current Account Total
1970	−34	−496	+462	+857	+823
1971	+190	−692	+882	+934	+1,124
1972	−748	−666	−82	+995	+247
1973	−2,586	−941	−1,645	+1,605	−981
1974	−5,351	−3,357	−1,994	+2,078	−3,273
1975	−3,333	−3,057	−276	+1,812	−1,521
1976	−3,927	−3,947	+20	+3,048	−879
1977	−2,278	−2,771	+493	+2,243	−35
1978	−1,573	−1,999	+426	+2,481	+908
1979	−3,497	−774	−2,723	+2,595	−902
1980	+1,177	+273	+904	+2,028	+3,205
1981	+3,360	+3,112	+148	+3,158	+6,528
1982	+2,331	+4,643	−2,312	+2,332	+4,663
1983	−835	+6,976	−7,811	+4,003	+3,168
1984	−4,101	+7,137	−11,238	+5,036	+935
1985	−2,068	+8,163	−10,231	+5,020	+2,952
1986	−8,463	+4,056	−12,519	+8,509	+46
1987	−10,929	+4,183	−15,112	+7,258	−3,671
1988	−20,815	+2,797	−23,612	+5,796	+15,019
1989	−23,112	+1,481	−24,593	+2,261	−20,851
1990	−18,675	+1,518	−20,193	+4,295	−14,380
1991	−10,284	+1,208	−11,492	+3,657	−6,627
1992	−13,406	+1,487	−14,893	+4,069	−9,337

SOURCES Central Statistical Office, *United Kingdom Balance of Payments*, 1983, 1985, 1993, CSO, London; Business Briefing (1992), *Balance of Payments*, 29 May, British Chambers of Commerce, Chester.

'First, the discovery of North Sea oil coincided roughly with the first oil price shock. Without oil, the UK would probably have needed to divert more resources to manufacturing in order to pay for the more expensive oil. Thus while the discovery of North Sea oil may entail a smaller manufacturing sector relative to an economy without oil, it need not imply a change in the historical trend when

*taken in conjunction with the increased price of oil. Thus we must
be careful to specify the reference point against which comparison
is made. Second, the policy environment must be clearly specified.
How would fiscal and monetary policy have differed if the economy
were without oil?'*

Furthermore, is the impact of oil seen as a short-run or long-run effect,
since temporary or permanent shocks may yield different results?

It is clear that between 1973 and 1981 the size of the manufacturing
sector fell by almost a fifth, while national income showed a modest rise
over that period. The great proportion of this decline is confined to the
1978–81 period during which there was a marked appreciation of both the
nominal and real exchange rates and which coincides with the the major
North Sea oil fields coming on stream and with the second oil price rise.
None the less, other factors too were changing in the economy. The same
period also saw the adoption of contractory fiscal and monetary policies
by the Thatcher Administration to control both inflation and the size of the
public sector. Thus these all played a contributory part in the demise of the
manufacturing sector and makes difficult the unravelling of the oil effect.

The revenue from oil, which has accrued mainly to the government, has
enabled it to increase government expenditure and/or to reduce taxes. Some
saw the oil revenues being frittered away on unemployment benefit as the
level of unemployment rose or to pay for a consumer spending spree rather
than being used for investment on capital projects. By the end of 1986,
between a third and a half of the economic rent from the North Sea had been
invested in overseas assets, yielding a substantial return in interests and dividends for the future. In fact, it could be argued that the income from North
Sea oil enabled the UK economy's income to remain at a fairly high level,
so the necessary structural changes could be made (see Table 2.6).

In terms of the balance of payments we have noted the important
contribution made by oil to the visible balance (see Chapter 4 for a more
derailed approach). This is the direct effect of North sea oil on the balance of
payments, but there are also indirect effects since the development of North
Sea oil required the importation of capital equipment, such as oil rigs, and a
significant fraction of this has been financed by inflows of foreign capital.

Does the development of a major resource lead to deindustrialisation,
that is a contraction of other exporting and import-substituting industries?
(Following Holland's experience with natural gas this is known as the
'Dutch disease'.) The Dutch disease can be seen clearly in the income or
wealth effects of having a natural resource. The argument is as follows:
having oil in sufficient quantities increases wealth which impacts on the
demand for consumer goods and the output from the service sector. If UK

TABLE 2.6
Net External Assets of Selected Countries ($bn)

	Average 1980–3	*1988*	*1989*
US			
$bn	107	−544	−674
Per cent of GNP	4	−11	−12
Per cent of exports	39	−126	−141
Japan			
$bn	20	291	307
Per cent of GNP	2	10	10
Per cent of exports	11	76	76
UK			
$bn	55	162	127
Per cent of GNP	12	19	16
Per cent of exports	44	83	73

SOURCES   Brittan, S. (1989) 'The True External Position', *The Financial Times*, 26 November; OECD, *World Economic Outlook*, 1993, table 75, OECD, Paris.

manufactures are good substitutes for world manufactures then the price of these is largely determined on the open market. In this case the price of services relative to manufactures will rise. If world manufactures are not good substitutes for domestic manufactures then the price of domestic manufactures will rise. This improvement in the terms of trade, the increased demand for services and the appreciation of the exchange rate are the main thrusts of the 'Dutch disease' argument. However, there is the resource effect argument. This suggests that if the level of output from the manufacturing sector is supplemented from the rest of the world but leaves that for services unaffected then the factor rewards that go to the service sector are improved. Factors move out of manufacturing and towards services, but not all factors are good substitutes between sectors so deindustrialisation occurs.

A main worry is that if the North Sea oil effect has led to a decline in the manufacturing sector, since oil is a finite resource what will happen when the oil runs out? To some extent it depends on how the revenue from oil is, and was, spent. If the revenues were mainly used to finance consumption or unemployment benefit then the process of deindustrialisation will need to be reversed in the future. Once export markets are lost, however, it may be difficult to retrieve them in the future. Moreover, the labour force may not possess the desired skills, especially if in the interim the economy has relied on low value-added sectors of production. Therefore, the temporary deindustrialisation of the economy owing partially to the impact of oil may have permanent effects on the competitiveness of British industry – the so-called hysteresis effect. Some of the oil revenue, as we have seen, has found its way into capital investment at home and overseas; thus when the oil runs out if the loss in revenue is matched by the revenue raised from these investments there will be no great changes in the economy.

In summary, the impact of North Sea oil is to some extent difficult to interpret. It would appear that it had a role to play in an appreciation of the exchange rate, making UK exports less competitive and imports more competitive. The windfall gain in foreign exchange that resulted from the positive balance on the oil account served also to expand the service sector and at the same time led to a decline in manufacturing. Whether the revenues from oil were used sensibly is open to question. With a rise in the level of unemployment some of the wealth generated from oil had to pay benefits to those who became unemployed; the remainder of the revenue has been invested, though whether this has been in order to help British industry is a moot point. So if oil cannot be 'blamed' outright, what other theories have been put forward to explain structural change in the UK economy?

The Stages of Growth Argument

As economies mature one feature is noticeable: the size of the industrial sector declines and the economy enters a post-industrial phase. Figure 2.2 shows the various development stages of an economy. The decline in the industrial sector occurs as market forces reallocate resources to reflect the different demand and supply conditions of a mature economy. Also, since labour productivity has generally grown faster in manufacturing compared with services, if demand conditions do not alter there will be a declining proportion of workers in the industrial sector. Moreover as incomes grow over time, the income elasticity of demand for services is greater than that for manufacturing and so there is a gradual move towards the service sector. Thus as an economy matures this theory suggests that a country will exhibit a reduced share of world manufacturing trade and increased import penetration from newly industrialised countries (NICs) in relatively labour-intensive manufactured products.

FIGURE 2.2
The Stages of Economic Growth

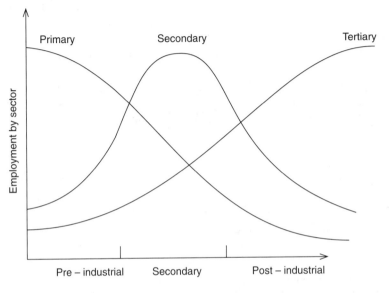

This stage-of-maturity argument is not convincing. For example, it cannot explain why the UK is deindustrialising faster than Japan or Germany which both have a higher GDP per head. Moreover, if the UK economy is becoming more mature, with increased desire for services, this does not appear to be reflected in the balance of payments since there is a continued desire for manufactured imports. Perhaps a stronger argument concerns the increased competition faced by the UK in low-cost manufactured goods from the NICs.

Low Wage Competition

One argument frequently cited is the fact that British goods are being undercut by cheaper imports from the NICs where employers pay lower wages to their employees, use less unionised or non-unionised labour and 'encourage' their workforce to work longer hours. It is often the case that lower wages in these NICs and less-developed countries (LDCs) are accompanied by lower productivity and lower-skilled workers.

If this is the situation facing the UK then it must be the same for other developed countries. Moreover, on the whole the UK could itself be seen

as a low-wage economy when compared with the major developed countries. Within this context it is important to bear in mind the role of the exchange rate. The appreciation of sterling at the end of the 1970s produced
a marked reduction in the price-competitiveness of British goods. In other
words, even though another country appears to be a lower-cost producer it
is possible to remain competitive via movements in the exchange rate.
Long-term changes of this type might also encourage foreign companies to
set up plants in another country.

   We should also consider the role of technology in trade. It is possible
that the UK could obtain its comparative advantage in textiles, which it
lost to low-wage producers in South-East Asia, if it invested in new levels
of technology. Non-price factors should also not be forgotten. It is widely
held that the unfavourable import and export elasticities faced by UK
manufacturing are as a result of poor quality goods and poor marketing
and the like (see Chapter 4).

The Role of Multinationals

When faced with uncompetitive conditions in the home economy multinational companies (MNCs) will often seek alternative foreign markets
which enable then to circumvent any trade barriers that they were facing
and also allows them to use their superior management, production techniques and technology to obtain the same, if not greater, revenue than they
were receiving in the home market.

   Multinational firms have traditionally been manufacturing firms rather
than service-orientated firms, and in the process of establishing themselves
in another country there will be a movement of jobs from the home to the
host economy. During the period 1972–83 nearly a third of all manufacturing jobs lost in the UK were from 58 British multinationals which created
200,000 jobs overseas. In addition to this effect, the UK has been one of the
countries which has benefited as a host economy from the growth in multinational activity. A danger with this scenario has been that when MNCs
rationalise their operations the UK may well lose jobs to other countries. An
example of this can be seen with the Ford operation in Europe who
transferred Sierra production out of the UK to mainland Europe.

   British multinationals could have a positive effect on industry in the UK
if, when they transfer some operations abroad creating extra jobs, the production of semi-raw materials and parts is left in the UK, thus creating
replacement and sometimes extra jobs at home as total UK multinational
output increases. None the less, MNCs can be blamed for the declining
share of some advanced countries in world manufacturing exports. For
example, it is possible that a another country's share of total world manu-

factures remains constant but that its overall control increases, not because it is producing more in its home economy but the production of these goods has shifted to lower-cost LDCs through the MNC activity. On a more positive note, MNCs may accelerate structural adjustment in an economy within the sector in which it is located. The MNC forces indigenous firms to compete and by investing in and reinforcing those sectors in which the country is most competitive, it can stimulate competitors and suppliers and aid the process of economic change in a positive way.

Crowding-out Revisited

If the theory of 'crowding-out' is to believed, it should not be country-specific; it appears that countries such as Italy and Germany have experienced substantial growth in their state sectors yet their share of world manufactures has hardly altered. For the UK in particular the 'crowding-out' theory seems inappropriate. It is argued that the UK has always possessed spare capacity both in labour and capital goods so that switching resources from the private to the public sector does not constrain the former but simply reduces the spare capacity, though there will still be some skill areas where excess demand has occurred.

There are also differences in the job market if we disaggregate the labour market by sex. Most manufacturing jobs were lost by males yet the growth of the state sector favoured female employment. Moreover, effective corporation tax appeared to fall during the 1970s and the Wilson Committee (*Report of the Committee to Review the Functioning of Financial Institutions*, Cmnd. 7937, London: HMSO, 1980) found that there had been no shortage of funds for British industry. There are also doubts relating to the years used in studies of the UK 'crowding-out' effects. If the years selected for the study do not correspond to the same points in the business cycle, comparisons are misleading.

Is it possible, however, that Bacon and Eltis's theory of 'crowding-out' is correct, not in the short run but over the longer term? If we roll-on the data and use Table 2.7 we can see that the rise of government-financed consumption has occurred at the same time as there has been a growth in marketed sector investment; in other words, successive Conservative Administrations have been unable to halt the growth of the non-marketed sector and the squeeze on profits most evident in the 1970s has been reversed. Therefore, even in the longer term, the Bacon and Eltis theory does not really stand up to scrutiny (see R. Bacon and W. Eltis, *Britain's Economic Problem: Too Few Producers*, 2nd edn London: Macmillan, 1976).

TABLE 2.7
The Long-run Relationship of the Marketed and Non-marketed Sectors (% of marketed output)

	1924	1937	1955	1965	1974	1979	1987
Marketed sector consumption	81.4	76.4	56.7	53.0	51.2	47.0	46.3
Marketed sector investment	6.5	9.4	14.0	17.3	19.0	19.7	17.3
Balance of trade	-3.0	-5.0	-1.8	-0.9	-6.1	0.2	-0.2
Government-financed consumption	9.3	9.8	20.3	18.8	22.1	21.8	25.0
Government purchases of materials and investment	5.8	9.5	10.7	11.7	13.8	11.3	11.2

SOURCES   Derived from Feinstein, C.H. (1972) *National Income, Expenditure and Output of the UK 1855–1965*, Cambridge University Press; Bacon, R. and Eltis, W.A. (1978) *Britain's Economic Problem: Too Few Producers*, 2nd edn, Macmillan; Central Statistical Office (1988) *UK National Accounts*, HMSO, London.

Perhaps, however, it is not the size of the state sector that is important but its composition. Is it possible that the UK with its high expenditure on defence, aerospace and high-profile products has diverted funds and high-quality labour away from other sectors and thus adversely affected the competitiveness of the private sector? For example, defence expenditure costs the UK about £20 billion per year, 10 per cent of all government expenditure. The evidence is not convincing, however: although the UK has one of the highest defence expenditure amongst its European neighbours at 5.1 per cent, there is no strict relationship between high defence expenditure and low economic growth. None the less, the British economy would benefit from cuts in defence spending through lower public expenditure, the release of scarce manpower, the switch of high-technology manufacturing capacity into civilian production, and a reduction in the military balance of payments.

Do Structural Changes Matter?

Structural changes in an economy are not new, but this chapter has highlighted the speed at which the manufacturing sector, in particular, collapsed from the mid-1970s. Conversely, the chapter also indicates the growth in the service sector and especially the growth of financial services. There is no single explanation as to why the UK has seen a decline in its manufacturing sector. Certainly, poor education of managers and workers, lack of R&D and the power of trade unions are contributory forces. None the less, the UK may well have received more losses than gains from the development of North Sea oil, certainly at the beginning of the 1980s. It also does not seem appropriate to consider the 'maturing economy' as an explanation of the UK's demise, since other countries should have experienced similar if not magnified problems from this source. The idea of crowding-out, the Bacon and Eltis argument, also does not seem to hold water in either the short or long term. There may be, therefore, some underlying forces in the UK economy which even 'Thatcherite policies' cannot alter.

In the short term, therefore, we have looked for ways of explaining the demise of the secondary sector in the UK and one of our 'escape clauses' is that the decline in the secondary sector does not matter since the service sector has grown to replace it in employment terms. But for how long can this trend continue? If the comparative advantage in services is also being lost is there any way back for manufacturing? But more fundamental than this is: do we really want a return of the manufacturing sector?.

Does Deindustrialisation Matter?

3

Whilst Chapter 2 described the main structural changes in the UK economy over the past 30 years this is certainly not the first time that the UK has been subject to changes of this type. The industrial revolution saw the decline in the agricultural sector and the subsequent growth in the secondary sector. The more recent process of deindustrialisation strikes a harsh note with many people, however, in that there is a decline in what many people see central to British society: manufacturing. Moreover, even though this decline has been gradual over the past century it has appeared to pick up speed during the 1970s and 1980s. Many other countries have seen similar trends to those experienced in the UK but our decline in the manufacturing sector seems more acute. As it declines it imposes a number of costs of adjustment on any society, such as regional and structural unemployment. Moreover, there is a view that without a sizeable manufacturing sector the balance of payments will always constrain the economy since it is unable to provide sufficient manufactured goods for its citizens. The size of the manufacturing sector may also have implications for an economy's growth, exchange rate, rate of interest, and inflation. Thus, is it possible for an economy to sustain itself by moving towards a post-industrial society or do we need to find some mechanism by which we can revive the manufacturing sector?

Definitions of Deindustrialisation

Deindustrialisation is an ambiguous term which means different things to different people. None the less, the following four definitions are those which might describe deindustrialisation within the UK:

1. Decline in employment, both in absolute and relative terms, in the manufacturing sector of the economy.
2. Decline in the share of national output contributed by the manufacturing sector of the economy.
3. Decline in Britain's share of world manufacturing output or world manufacturing exports.
4. Failure, due to poor export performance and/or increased import penetration, to generate sufficient exports to finance a full-employment level of imports.

In addition to these, the definition of deindustrialisation must be one which enables us to compare one country with another and it should also be 'cause-free': it should not predetermine its causes.

Deindustrialisation may occur if we do not possess an efficient manufacturing sector which not only satisfies the demands of consumers at home but also enables us to sell enough of our products abroad to pay for the nation's imports. Moreover, this efficient manufacturing sector should be able to attain these objectives with acceptable levels of output, employment and a satisfactory exchange rate. If these factors are not met then a country is suffering from deindustrialisation, and accordingly the UK fits into this category.

As an example of this, consider the UK economy, first, at the end of the 1980s and, secondly, at the beginning of the 1990s. In the late 1980s the UK's visible trade balance reached a deficit of £24.5 billion, and was symptomatic of a country in which consumers' expenditure was buoyant and where consumers were either not able to purchase home-produced goods or preferred to purchase foreign imports. In fact this figure would have been far worse if there had not been surpluses both on the oil account and for invisibles. In the early 1990s, however, the picture was somewhat different: the balance of trade deficit was much reduced, to between £9–13 billion, though at the cost of the UK going into recession. In other words, increases in aggregate demand tend to cause the UK's balance of payments to tip further into the red. This decline in the balance of payments acts as a constraint on government macroeconomic policy which, it was hoped, the development of North Sea oil would remove. If we now add the fact that UK output and employment are also not at 'acceptable' levels, then the UK fits squarely into the definition of deindustrialisation suggested above. However, this definition of deindustrialisation would leave most non-oil-producing industrial countries categorised as deindustrialised since their dependence on oil has left their economies constrained by their balance of payments following the oil price hikes of 1973–74 and 1979. None the less, this definition highlights the importance of the balance of payments in the deindustrialisation debate.

Bacon and Eltis's Theory of Deindustrialisation

We have seen the Bacon and Eltis arguments for 'crowding-out' in Chapter 2. In their view, the non-market sectors use resources and generate income but do not provide any output to the market. The resources for these sectors must come from somewhere, and an easy source of supply is the market sector. If the market sector is to forgo some of its claims on its own output then a tax system could provide this facility; in doing so these resources are channelled into the non-market sector. Suppose, however, that the market sector or the government does not accommodate the claims by the non-market sector on the market sector. What then? In an open economy adjustments must be made externally, either by diverting the exports of the market sector to the home economy or by increasing imports, or by a combination of the two. Whichever method occurs we shall see a deterioration in the balance of payments. Once again the balance of payments constraint will lead to a deterioration in economic growth with a possible increase in the rate of interest, higher taxation and further knock-on effects to wages, competitiveness and inflation. Thus in this way the non-market public sector has 'crowded-out' the market sector and hampered the UK's economic performance. However, where there are unemployed resources or where resources are growing it is quite possible for the non-market sector to be expanding whilst at the same time the manufacturing sector is growing and, as we have seen already in Chapter 2, there are reasons to doubt whether the Bacon and Eltis theory is a good explanation of the deindustrialisation faced by the UK economy during the 1980s.

OECD Definitions

The OECD definitions of deindustrialisation which are cause-free and not time- and place-specific use one or both of the following to define deindustrialisation:

1. a declining share of total employment in manufacturing; and
2. an absolute decline in employment in manufacturing.

As Tables 3.1 and 3.2 indicate, the developing economies generally and the UK economy in particular have experienced a declining share of civilian employment in manufacturing.

In the UK the fall in the demand for labour is associated with a reduction in output until 1987 and probably a rise in the wage level relative to

TABLE 3.1
Employees in Employment by Industry in the UK (thousands)[a]

	1971	1979	1981	1983	1986	1988[b]	1993
Manufacturing							
Extraction of minerals and ores other than fuels, manufacture of metal, mineral products, and chemicals	1,282	1,147	939	817	729	688	599
Metal goods, engineering, and vehicle industries	3,709	3,374	2,923	2,548	2,372	2,366	1,898
Other	3,074	2,732	2,360	2,159	2,126	2,168	1,693
Total manufacturing	8,065	7,253	6,222	5,525	5,227	5,222	4,190
Services							
Distribution, hotels, catering, and repairs	3,686	4,257	4,172	4,118	4,298	4,442	4,549
Transport and communication	1,556	1,479	1,425	1,345	1,298	1,326	1,281
Banking, finance, insurance, business services, and leasing	1,336	1,647	1,739	1,875	2,166	2,475	2,629
Other	5,049	6,197	6,132	6,163	6,536	6,966	7,036
Total services	11,627	13,580	13,468	13,501	14,297	15,210	15,495
Agriculture, forestry, and fishing	450	380	363	350	329	313	260
Energy and water supply industries	798	722	710	648	545	487	357
Construction	1,198	1,239	1,130	1,044	989	1,044	831
All industries and services	22,139	23,173	21,892	21,067	21,387	22,276	21,133

NOTES
[a] As at June each year.
[b] The effect of revisions undertaken in 1991 impacted primarily on the 1989 and 1990 data.
SOURCES *Social Trends*, no. 21 (1991 edn), table 4.11; *Employment Gazette*, April 1991; Jan. 1994.

TABLE 3.2
Changes in the Labour Force: Selected Countries (%)

	France	Germany	Japan	UK	USA
1950					
Agriculture	27.4	23.2	41.0	4.9	11.9
Industry	37.0	44.4	24.2	49.4	35.9
Services	35.6	32.4	34.8	45.7	52.2
1970					
Agriculture	13.9	8.6	17.4	3.2	4.5
Industry	39.7	48.5	35.7	44.8	34.4
Services	46.4	42.9	46.9	52.0	61.1
1990					
Agriculture	6.1	3.4	7.2	2.1	2.8
Industry	30.0	39.7	34.1	28.8	26.2
Services	63.9	56.9	58.7	69.1	70.9

SOURCES   Bairoch, P. (1968), *La Population Active et Sa Structure*,
Brussels, OECD; Organisation for Economic Co-operation and
Development (1991) *Labour Force Statistics*, Paris.

the price of other factors. Some of the decline in manufacturing employment was to be expected, however, since we had passed the peak of production from North Sea oil and gas. Table 3.1 also indicates that there has been a change in the industrial structure of UK industry. In fact, by 1993 there were almost exactly the same number of employees in employment as in 1971; however, the manufacturing sector had shrunk by almost 4 million, whilst the service sector had increased by 3.8 million. We should not think that all elements of the service sector have benefited from the growth in employment. As Table 3.3 shows, it is the financial services sector, that is banking and finance, insurance, business services and the like, which have been the major beneficiaries of the boom in service employment. Areas such as transport and communications have shown a relative decline.

The absolute decline in manufacturing employment means that its share of total employment has also declined over time, especially if employment in other sectors is growing faster, or contracting at a slower rate. To put this fact into perspective, the financial and business services sector were the fastest-growing sectors of the economy in the 1980s. Their output doubled, with an average real growth rate of over 7 per cent. One reason for this was the demise of other sectors of the economy, but this sector

TABLE 3.3
Growth of Financial Services in Great Britain

	1975		1979		1985		1989		1993	
	No. employed (000s)	Per cent of total employment	No. employed (000s)	Per cent of total employment	No. employed (000s)	Per cent of total employment	No. employed (000s)	Per cent of total employment	No. employed (000s)	Per cent of total employment
Wholesale distribution and repairs	1,032	4.6	1,111	4.9	1,148	5.5	1,206	5.4	1,062	5.1
Retail dist.	2,050	9.2	2,135	9.4	2,038	9.7	2,234	10.1	2,221	10.7
Hotel and catering	824	3.7	931	4.1	1,027	4.9	1,198	5.4	1,177	5.7
Transport	1,041	4.7	1,044	4.6	889	4.2	902	4.1	883	4.2
Postal services and telecom.	439	2.0	414	1.8	419	2.0	438	2.0	373	1.8
Banking, finance, insurance, business services and leasing	1,468	6.6	1,622	7.2	2,039	9.7	2,594	11.7	2,577	12.4
Public admin.	1,937	8.7	1,947	8.6	1,862	8.9	1,870	8.4	1,814	8.7
Education	1,534	6.9	1,605	7.1	1,557	7.4	1,721	7.7	1,832	8.8
Medical and other health services	1,112	5.0	1,190	5.3	1,301	6.2	1,418	6.4	1,538	7.4
Other services	1,108	5.0	1,262	5.6	1,489	7.1	1,680	7.6	1,713	8.2

SOURCE *Employment Gazette*, 1994.

also benefited from changes in government policy which liberalised financial services. Employment in financial and business services rose from 7 to 12 per cent of total UK employment between 1979 and 1990, whilst at the same time employment in manufacturing fell from 31 to 22 per cent (see Table 3.3). It is doubtful whether the positive trend in the financial services sector can continue into the future since the liberalisation of financial services may have given just a 'one-off' boost. Thus, although financial and business services helped to raise the UK's GDP growth rate from 1.8 to 2.3 per cent in the 1980s, it cannot be relied on to do so in the 1990s, and therefore there is all the more reason to be concerned about deindustrialisation in the manufacturing sector.

The decline in the manufacturing sector, however, is not a singularly British phenomenon but one that has been occurring in most developing economies over the last 30 years. However, it does seem more marked in Britain than elsewhere. It may well be that the process of deindustrialisation started earlier in Britain since Britain was the first industrialised country and we would expect other countries to catch up. Such an argument appears to have some support if we look at the share of manufacturing in GDP (see Table 3.4).

For all countries there appears to be a decline in manufacturing as a share of GDP; however, this proportional decline in output is not necessarily an indication of an ailing manufacturing sector since part of the decline will be due to a fall in the price of manufactures relative to the price of goods and services generally. Of more concern from a UK point of view is its general decline in its percentage of world manufacturing

TABLE 3.4
Share of Manufacturing in GDP

	1960	*1970*	*1975*	*1980*	*1986*	*1991*
USA	28.6	25.7	23.4	22.5	19.9	19.6
Japan	33.9	35.9	29.9	30.4	29.3	29.7
France	29.1	28.7	27.4	26.3	22.2	21.3
West Germany	40.3	38.4	34.5	33.0	33.1	31.9
Italy	28.5	28.9	29.7	30.5	23.4	22.4
UK	32.1	28.1	26.3	23.1	21.8	20.9

SOURCES   Organisation for Economic Co-operation and Development (1988) *National Accounts of OECD Countries*, Paris; World Bank (1993) *Economic Outlook*, New York.

TABLE 3.5
World Trade Shares and Deindustrialisation (%)

| | *Shares of World Trade in Manufactures* | | | | | |
	1950	*1960*	*1970*	*1979*	*1990*	*1991*
France	9.9	9.6	8.7	10.5	9.7	10
Germany	7.3	19.3	19.8	20.9	20.2	20
Japan	3.4	6.9	11.7	13.7	15.9	17
UK	25.5	16.5	10.8	9.1	8.6	9
USA	27.3	21.6	18.6	16.0	16.0	18

SOURCES   Bairoch (1968); OECD (1991), National Institute of Economic and Social Research (1970, 1983); *UN Monthly Bulletin of Statistics* (1990); OECD (1992).

trade, a characteristic not shown by other major trading nations, as Table 3.5 indicates.

We should not conclude from the above analysis that that an absolute decline in employment in manufacturing is an indication of the continued downward slide of the UK economy. It is possible that technology in manufacturing is reducing employment in this sector whilst at the same time raising overall productivity. Moreover, technology can be market-extending as it creates new products, allows entry into new markets and generally makes an uncompetitive industry a price-competitive one. The measures of deindustrialisation should also not be taken in isolation, because doing so will result in a partial view of the problem. For example, the output measure does not take into account changes in population: industrial output per capita may show greater or less deindustrialisation. Moreover, the measurement of services in particular is sensitive to the way in which they are defined and whether these are valued by volume or value, etc. For example, the higher growth contribution of manufacturing compared with services can be reversed if we change the basis for the calculation. In addition, government statistics classify firms according to their primary activity, so that if a manufacturing firm uses an outside contractor for its accountancy or design functions – tasks which it used to undertake in-house – then there will be a fall in manufacturing employment and a corresponding rise in service sector employment. In fact as a firm grows the proportion of its workforce devoted to production may fall quite substantially. Thus, far from being a manufacturing company, it would be better designated a service company.

Positive and Negative Impacts of Deindustrialisation

Deindustrialisation has become a popular discussion point within the UK economy since there is a view that manufacturing makes a more fundamental and basic contribution to the economy than the various service industries. This argument has led to much heated debate; however, before examining this point let us look at deindustrialisation itself. Is it always 'bad'? It is possible that we may get positive deindustrialisation. Such a situation occurs when, although there is a relative decline in the importance of manufacturing, the health of this sector is improved provided it continues to grow in absolute terms, to maintain full employment and to produce enough export goods to balance a country's desire for imports. Or, put another way, if employment is falling but output still proceeds to grow at a high rate due to productivity increases, this may not be a major cause for concern especially if the displaced labour is absorbed into the non-manufacturing sector. Moreover, if this is also linked to increased leisure time and a fall in the working life of those employed in this sector, then the process may be a positive aspect of a maturing economy.

Negative deindustrialisation, on the other hand, occurs when industry declines to such an extent that it prevents the government of a country achieving its economic goals. In terms of the UK, the period since the 1960s has been one of negative deindustrialisation on a large scale with a decline in the share of manufacturing employment and output as a proportion of total activity, coupled with one of the slowest rates of growth of a developed nation.

These positive and negative aspects of deindustrialisation can be seen in Figure 3.1. Suppose the economy is at X; now a process of deindustrialisation occurs and those workers displaced from the manufacturing sector find alternative employment in the non-manufacturing or service sector. The economy therefore, still remains at full employment and the GDP per capita has increased. This movement from X to Y is positive deindustrialisation. If, however, we again start at A and now move to Z, that is, the share of manufacturing employment has fallen but at the same time so has GDP per capita, then this is a process of negative deindustrialisation.

Given that the UK has experienced bouts of negative deindustrialisation, some of them severe, the burdens of these have not been equally borne by all sectors of society because the deindustrialisation process has hit certain geographical regions and certain industrial sectors more harshly than others.

FIGURE 3.1
Positive and Negative Deindustrialisation

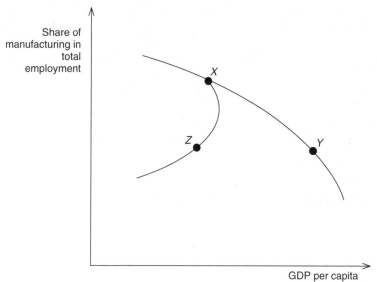

The Regional Dimension of Deindustrialisation

Until the end of the 1970s deindustrialisation was a problem the UK appeared to be able to live with. Declining industrial unemployment was almost compensated for by replacement jobs in the service sector. This position ended after 1980 leading to an overall rise in unemployment. The costs of this deindustrialisation and its severe adjustment problems were more pronounced in regions where there was a heavy concentration of declining industries, such as the West Midlands, the North, Yorkshire and Humberside, the North-West, Wales and Scotland. During the 1980s these areas all experienced unemployment levels above the national average (around 10 per cent). Moreover, the boom in the UK at the end of the 1980s still left these regions worse off than others. By contrast the South-East of England faired much better, since over 70 per cent of employees were in the service industries; though once again not all service industries have boomed during the 1980s as much as hotels, catering and financial services: employment has actually fallen in transport, postal and tele-communications services.

This restructuring of the industrial base cannot be explained solely by deindustrialisation. The East Midlands, for example, which is also heavily dependent on manufacturing, did not experience the same sort of problems as those being faced by its neighbour in the West. In other words, it may not be simply a case of all industries declining, but just specific ones.

A clear picture of the changes in the economy can only be seen if we look at disaggregated data. Trends in output and employment, profit records, the level of spare capacity, and the like, all provide indications of how well the different sectors of industry are performing. In the UK it would appear that mechanical engineering, motor manufacture and textiles have been declining rapidly whilst the electrical engineering sector and chemicals have performed well (see Figure 3.2).

FIGURE 3.2
Visible Balance of Commodity Groups, 1980 and 1988

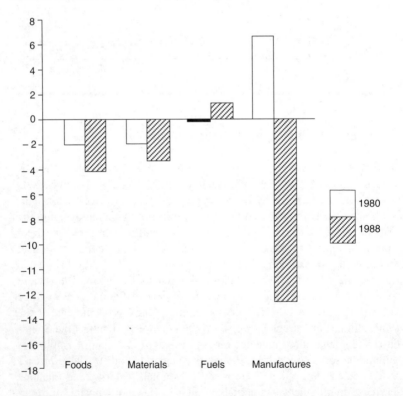

SOURCE   CSO.

Often the industries in decline are the old-established ones while the new high-tech industries are in the ascendancy. For example, in the US while the volume of other exports fell by 10 per cent from 1981–5, the volume of high-tech exports rose by 30 per cent. However, even with traditional industries regeneration is possible due to the impact of new production techniques or higher levels of technology.

Turning once more to the regional dimension of deindustrialisation in the UK, it proves difficult to concentrate on the Thatcher decade without making reference to the North–South divide. If this divide is present then it has had adverse effects on the performance of the national economy and on the government's macroeconomic policies. The regional imbalances and impact of regional deindustrialisation have their lineage in the different industrial structures that have existed historically in the regions.

Table 3.6 indicates those areas that had performed badly in the past were the ones to bear the brunt of the major restructuring that occurred through deindustrialisation. Between 1971 and 1979 the North saw 493,000 jobs lost in manufacturing (11 per cent) compared with a loss of 299,000(8.7 per cent) in the South of the country: mostly in London. East Anglia, the East Midlands and the South-West increased their manufacturing employment.

Government policy to regenerate employment in the North by encouraging firms to develop or relocate there also had important consequences for the Midlands, which was being bypassed as an investment region. In contrast to the 1970s, the 1980s saw an even further deterioration in the manufacturing sector in all regions except East Anglia. Once again the North–South divide was in evidence but this time it was more pronounced. Between 1979 and 1988 the North lost 1.386 million jobs (34.3 per cent) in manufacturing whilst the South lost 726,000 (23.2 per cent). To some extent these figures are not surprising since some saw the North as an area of older declining industries where unions were less flexible and workers less productive, whilst the South had a greater incidence of younger manufacturing industries, which were more efficient and had more flexible workforces.

The government were blamed for exacerbating the problems. In the recession of the early 1980s they introduced a series of tight monetary and fiscal policies which aided the decline in manufacturing. Moreover, the rationalisation of production by multinational companies spurred on by the abolition of exchange controls and the deflationary squeeze in the UK economy also led to the transfer abroad of a number of manufacturing jobs. The government's policy of privatisation can also be held partly to blame for the decline of manufacturing employment. Newly privatised industries, free from the shackles of government control and spurred on by

TABLE 3.6
Uneven Geography of Economic Restructuring, 1971–9 and 1979–88

	Change in the Number of Employees in Employment in Manufacturing and Services							
	Percentage change				Absolute change (000s)			
	1971–9		1979–88		1971–9		1979–88	
	Manufacturing	Services	Manufacturing	Services	Manufacturing	Services	Manufacturing	Services
South-East	-15.2	10.7	-29.4	14.9	-336	489	-550	750
East Anglia	7.2	27.2	5.8	33.3	14	86	12	134
South-West	3.8	34.5	-17.1	10.9	16	256	-75	109
East Midlands	1.0	34.3	-18.6	22.2	7	192	-113	167
'South'	-8.7	16.6	-23.2	16.1	-299	1023	-726	1160
West Midlands	-11.0	17.90	-29.3	15.8	-122	163	-228	169
Yorkshire–Humberside	-9.2	22.2	-37.4	14.4	-72	190	-265	151
North-West	-15.9	11.6	-38.2	-2.2	-184	155	-371	-33
Northern	-7.7	13.7	-36.3	9.2	-14	80	-149	61
Wales	-2.8	21.1	-32.4	2.5	-9	106	-102	-2
Scotland	-11.9	14.4	-36.3	5.6	-72	171	-219	68
'North'	-11.0	16.5	-34.8	7.4	-493	859	-1386	451
Great Britain	-10.0	16.5	-29.7	12.0	-792	1882	2112	1611

NOTES (1) Changes calculated from mid-year to mid-year; (2) comparable data for Northern Ireland not available.
SOURCE Department of Employment.

the need to be lean and efficient, began to off-load some of their manufacturing employment.

The decline in manufacturing employment, it has been argued, has been
compensated for by the rise in service industry employment, yet this too
has its spatial dimensions. Far from looking at the arguments as to whether
service industry growth can fill the gap left by the decline of manufacturing or as to the UK's share of world invisible exports (this is looked at
elsewhere), the growth in the UK service industry appeared to be evenly
spread amongst the regions during the period 1971–9. The picture during
the 1980s is somewhat different. Whereas during the 1970s public sector
service employment was one of the areas that soaked up the loss in manufacturing jobs, the decade of the 1980s was the period of growth of private
sector services which was uneven across the country. Between 1979 and
1988 there was over double the proportion of service industry jobs created
in the South compared with the North. Thus there is an inverse relationship between deindustrialisation and the growth of the service sector
during the 1980s. This fact is not altogether surprising since service jobs
are to some extent complementary to manufacturing jobs. Moreover, as
the Northern regions declined in manufacturing employment so did the
level of income in these regions, thus they were not conducive to the expansion of services. In addition we should not overlook the role of the
City of London in the South's figures for the service industry and the location of two important growth areas in East Anglia and the South-West,
which could offer suitable sites for service industry development.

Finally, even though the South was the main beneficiary of these new
service industry jobs we need to consider how many were actual full-
time/high-wage jobs rather than temporary/low paid work.

Growth and the Manufacturing Sector

The importance of the manufacturing sector in the growth process lies in
the fact that it is here that most of the increases in productivity can be
achieved. Technological improvements, which permit a greater volume of
output to be achieved from a given volume of inputs, although a possibility in the primary and tertiary sectors, are much more easily achieved
in the manufacturing sector. Other things being equal, the larger the size of
the secondary sector in relation to the primary and tertiary sectors the
larger is the scope for productivity gains and hence for growth. This move
towards a rise in the tertiary sector is usually well under way as an
economy matures but, in the UK's case, it was suggested that the burgeon-
ing service sector swallowed up resources before a high level of output per

head could be achieved; thus the UK was suffering from 'premature maturity'. Kaldor's ideas on growth throw further light on the issues. First, there is a strong positive relationship between the growth of manufacturing industry and the growth rate of the economy as a whole. Secondly, there is a strong positive correlation between the growth of manufacturing output and the rate of growth of productivity in manufacturing(see Verdoorn's Law in Chapter 1). Thirdly, since resources are scarce, if they are used in manufacturing, where productivity levels are higher than in any other sector, there is a strong positive relationship between the rate at which manufacturing output and employment grows and the rate at which productivity grows outside manufacturing (see N. Kaldor, *Causes of the Slow Rate of Economic Growth of the United Kingdom* Cambridge: Cambridge University Press, 1968). Point three suggests that if we increase employment growth in any other sector other than the secondary sector then we shall slow up overall productivity growth. If we put all three points together, a country which has a higher rate of growth in manufacturing output than another will have higher productivity growth which, because of economies of scale, will make its goods more price-competitive; thus demand for its goods rises, inducing further productivity growth, and so on. Of course, like any upward spiral there is also a down-side to this hypothesis, and so if the UK has low economic growth it means low productivity growth, an output which is less price-competitive, a reduced demand for labour, etc. So if we wish the economy to grow at a higher level we require a sufficiently large manufacturing sector.

There is some debate, however, as to whether Verdoorn's Law only applies to manufacturing since the data from 1972 to 1986 suggest that it applies equally to a large section of the service sector. The problem lies with separating productive processes from service processes. The complete process by which raw materials are transformed into finished products goes through many stages in which a large proportion of the work is undertaken by the service sector, such as transportation. Moreover, the leasing of plant from service sector organisations also became a growing phenomenon during the 1980s. In fact, the tendency for manufacturing companies to devolve activities, like sales, marketing, distribution, to specialist service concerns has accounted for around half the shift of manufacturing jobs to the service industry. What we should be dealing with are two branches of services: those that are marketed and those that are not. The principal services which play no part in the productive process(non-marketed services) are often those provided by the state. One estimate is that of the workers who shifted from the productive and construction industries during the period from 1971 to 1986 two-thirds went on to produce marketed services that were either complementary to manufacturing or else tradable for manufactures. It follows that there is no *a priori* reason to suppose that this shift from manufacturing to marketable services involved any weakening in the ability of the UK economy to finance its necessary imports and to provide the capital equipment from domestic and overseas sources that is indispensable to economic growth.

Balance of Payments Constrained Growth

During the years when the UK had its fastest growth rate, 1951–73, export growth was still lower than that of countries such as Germany and France. It is possible to conclude from this result that the British growth rate was constrained by its balance of payments. In other words, except where the balance of payments equilibrium growth rate exceeds the maximum feasible capacity growth rate, the rate of growth of a country will approximate to the ratio of its rate of growth of exports and its income elasticity of demand for imports. The question that needs to be asked here is: what are the elasticities of demand for imports and exports for various countries and can we work out the balance of payments constrained growth rate? To answer the second part of the question first, if we assume that there is little variation in the relative prices of imports and exports, then changes in these are responses to income variations both within and outside the country. In this case there will be a level of domestic income which just keeps the growth of imports in line with the growth of exports. This growth of income which will give us a balance of payments equilibrium on the current account will just equal the rate of growth of export volume divided by the income elasticity of demand for imports. This is the so-called balance of payments constrained growth rate, which can be seen in Figure 3.3.

The figure shows two levels of export growth, X_a and X_b, with $X_a>X_b$, and two levels of import growth M_a and M_b, and again $M_a>M_b$. Since $M_a>M_b$ we say that M_a has the greater income elasticity of demand. Thus in the diagram we can see that there are a number of possible equilibrium positions which would establish for us the GDP growth rate consistent with a balance of payments equilibrium. For example, a country with a low export growth rate (X_b) and a high income elasticity of demand for imports (M_a) would obtain equilibrium at S. Empirical evidence seems to suggest the following: no country can have a growth rate over the long term which is inconsistent with balance of payment equilibrium on the current account. If a country wishes to grow at a much higher rate, it must pursue a target of export growth through either productivity gains or

FIGURE 3.3
The Balance of Payments Constrained Growth Rate

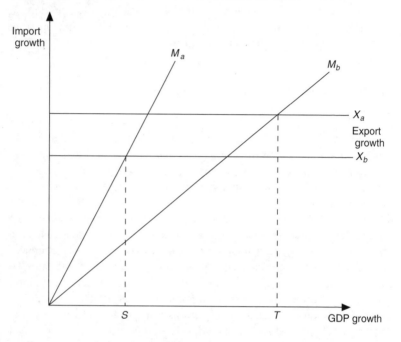

through lower prices, or it may seek policies to constrain imports such as barriers to trade or a tight fiscal policy. However, simply making goods more price competitive may not be enough since it is possible that non-price factors, such as quality, after-sales service, delivery on time, are much more important to consumers in export markets.

To return to the first half of the question asked above, can we ascertain the various elasticities of demand for imports and exports? There is some suggestion that estimates of income elasticities of demand for exports and imports are a little unreliable. Some suggest that the UK income elasticity values are lower than those obtained for France and Germany, whilst others found the reverse to be true. In the case of price elasticities of demand, there are difficulties in obtaining an accurate measurement, but the indications are that UK exports are more responsive to price than are UK imports, though even here there is no clear agreement as to whether price plays a dominant or a secondary role in the demand for manufactures.

If the manufacturing sector is in retreat, can the service sector come to its rescue, and in doing so resolve the problems with the balance of payments? A difficulty here is that not all services can be traded internationally (e.g. public sector services); as a result the trade in manufactures exceeds greatly the trade in services. Moreover, the UK does not possess a comparative advantage in all areas of the service sector, that is in sea transport, civil aviation, travel, general government services and financial and business services. It is only in the latter where a consistent surplus still exists, and this is in decline. To reiterate a point made earlier, the service sector should not be judged independently of the manufacturing sector, since the service sector is heavily dependent on computer technology and know-how, which we may need to import. Much more striking is the fact that the House of Lords Select Committee in 1985 pointed out that a 3 per cent rise in services exports is required to offset a 1 per cent fall in manufacturing exports. More worrying is that the market for financial services is becoming much more competitive, and one in which the level of competition will further increase in the Single European market(SEM). Even before entering the SEM the surplus on financial and banking services rose from 1.9 per cent of GDP in 1980 to 2.8 per cent in 1986–7, but fell to 2.0 per cent in 1992. Thus even if services could be the saviour of the balance of payments their prospects for the future are not good.

Manufacturing's Future Return?

'We must have a concerted campaign to promote greater esteem for the manufacturing industry. ... Only a substantial increase in manufacturing output can correct the huge deficit on our balance of trade.' (House of Lords Select Committee on Science and Technology, *Innovation in Manufacturing Industry*, London: HMSO, 1991)

Whichever definition we take, the UK has been suffering from deindustrialisation. The importance of the manufacturing sector as one which underpins UK productivity, growth, inflation and balance of trade is paramount. None the less, there are those who suggest that the service sector can provide much of the impetus for the achievement of these macroeconomic goals. A third view is that the service sector can provide some but not all the necessary stimulus for the economy and that the manufacturing sector must be made more competitive by various supply-side measures and the like (see Chapter 6). Some argue that the supply-side measures are working, since the latest figures for the UK's percentage of world manufactures have shown a modest increase, though how much of this is due to the impact of foreign multinational manufacturing growth in the UK is open to question. Thus the return of the manufacturing sector is a possibility, except that on this occasion the ownership and control may be disproportionately in the hands of foreign owners.

Does Slow Growth Matter?

A high level of growth has been one of the goals of successive governments throughout the last century, but in a world where population growth is still very high, particularly in the less developed countries, and where developed nations are not the most efficient users of finite resources, then the 'going for growth' campaign is now subject to a number of qualifications. Countries are beginning to turn towards the idea of constrained growth, particularly those which are currently in the leading pack of industrial nations. But there are some just outside this group and others from less developed countries which feel that if they are to make up any ground in the world's pecking order they must continue to strive for the highest growth rate possible, even though finite resources may be used up more rapidly, or that this growth may result in greater negative externalities. In other words, growth may well bring benefits to an individual country but the cost to the rest of the world may be excessive.

The Benefits of Growth

The benefits an economy can obtain from growth are numerous. For many Third World countries economic growth is a necessity if they are to remove mass poverty. For developed nations the case is less clear-cut. Certainly there can be major advantages from growth since the majority of the population wants higher real incomes. None the less there are important disadvantages outlined later which question the goal of maximising growth.

On the positive side we have seen already that growth allows a country the resources to undertake further investment programmes, to increase R&D, to raise economic productivity and thereby improve the balance of payments. Provided economic growth outstrips population growth, it will lead to higher real incomes per head of population. This can lead to higher levels of consumption of goods and services and higher welfare. Without growth in productive potential, people's increasing demands for real income growth are likely to lead to higher inflation, balance of payments crises (due to the rise in demand for imports), industrial unrest, and so on. Growth in this case helps to meet people's aspirations and in doing so avoids the macroeconomic crises that slow or zero growth would bring. In addition, as real incomes grow then from the increased tax revenue the government can redistribute income from the rich to the poor without the rich losing out absolutely. Without a continued rise in national income the scope for helping the poor is much more limited. A richer society achieved through the mechanism of growth has time to devote to more leisure activities and may become more concerned with the environment. Thus as an economy grows it can afford to care more for the environment by tackling the externalities that arise through production.

Growth is also seen as a way of eliminating poverty, though this is debatable and depends upon whether poverty is a relative or absolute term. It should be noted that the poor who often depend for their incomes on what the government gives them are the members of society least likely to benefit from the 'trickle-down' effect from economic growth. Finally, as economic growth increases income per capita rises and overall mortality decreases.

In the UK context, however, going for growth has had its problems. High growth has tended to drag in imports and upset the external balance. This has led to a series of 'stop–go' cycles in the UK economy and instability that has inhibited long-term investment in manufacturing. As Thirlwall notes, 'before short term capacity growth is reached, then demand must be curtailed, capacity is never fully utilised, investment is discouraged, technological progress is slowed down, and a country's goods compared with foreign goods become less desirable, so worsening the balance of payments still further' (A.P. Thirlwall, 'The Balance of Payments and Economic Performance', *National Westminster Bank Quarterly Review* (May 1992) pp. 2–11). Given the decline in the UK's manufacturing sector, some would argue that the balance of payments is acting during the 1990s even more as a 'governor on the economy' than it did a decade earlier.

Growth and the External Constraint

It has been shown earlier (Chapters 1 and 2) that the manufacturing sector has declined appreciably over the past three decades whilst there has been a major growth in the services sector in general and the financial services sector in particular. The decline in manufacturing and the growth in services is important from the point of view of the UK's trading performance. It is estimated that only 20 per cent of service activities are tradable compared with virtually all of manufactured goods. This is still true even when we consider that many service activities are related to areas of production. Thus deindustrialisation matters because of its effects on the balance of payments. Although the UK's balance of invisible trade has been in deficit for most of the last century, historically this has not presented a major problem since the surplus on the invisibles account more than off-set this. Since 1945, however, the export competitiveness of the UK's non-oil exportables has fallen and at the same time there has been a rise in import penetration.

Table 4.1 shows the overall picture for the UK's current account between 1970 and 1992. It indicates the strength of the invisible account, though the health of this sector has come under pressure during the late 1980s and early 1990s as competition in this area increased. For example, Britain's share of world exports of services has fallen back from 12 per cent in 1970 to around 7 per cent in the early 1990s.

The table also shows the importance of oil in the visible balance, its rise during the early 1980s and subsequent decline, and also the growing trend of the non-oil account to go into deficit. The £24 billion deficit in 1989 has been reduced to under £10 billion in 1991–2 but at a cost of negative growth and high unemployment. The current account has been roughly in balance only twice since the late 1970s: in 1977 and 1986. The large surplus in the early 1980s was caused as much by the effect on imports of the 1980–1 recession as by rising net exports of North Sea oil, which did not reach their peak until 1985. The 1989 deficit was caused by the reverse: excess domestic demand satisfied by purchasing imports as well as the decline of the oil surplus.

Why, therefore, has the UK's non-oil balance deteriorated, why have the patterns of trade by commodity and country altered over time, and to what extent does the manufacturing sector play its part in these changes?

If we take the non-oil visible balance, the deficits and surpluses have tended to follow the business cycle with deficits occurring during boom periods as the UK economy has sucked in imports and surpluses when the economy has been in recession. Mini booms in the economy during 1973–4 and 1978–9 can also be seen in the figures. Since 1980 the picture has changed to some extent with the non-oil visible balance deteriorating considerably even though the economy has faced booms and recessions. Moreover, if we take the figures from 1986 onwards the deficit has worsened still further as it was fuelled by the 'Lawson' consumer boom. The problems with the visible account could be a reflection of a number of

TABLE 4.1
The UK's Balance of Trade

Year	Visible Balance Total	Oil	Non-oil	Invisible Balance Total	Current Account Total
1970	−34	−496	+462	+857	+823
1971	+190	−692	+882	+934	+1,124
1972	−748	−666	−82	+995	+247
1973	−2,586	−941	−1,645	+1,605	−981
1974	−5,351	−3,357	−1,994	+2,078	−3,273
1975	−3,333	−3,057	−276	+1,812	−1,521
1976	−3,927	−3,947	+20	+3,048	−879
1977	−2,278	−2,771	+493	+2,243	−35
1978	−1,573	−1,999	+426	+2,481	+908
1979	−3,497	−774	−2,723	+2,595	−902
1980	+1,177	+273	+904	+2,028	+3,205
1981	+3,360	+3,112	+148	+3,168	+6,528
1982	+2,331	+4,643	−2,312	+2,332	+4,663
1983	−835	+6,975	−7,811	+4,003	+3,168
1984	−4,101	+7,137	−11,238	+5,036	+935
1985	−2,068	+8,163	−10,231	+5,020	+2,952
1986	−8,463	+4,056	−12,519	+8,509	+46
1987	−10,929	+4,183	−15,112	+7,258	−3,671
1988	−20,815	+2,797	−23,612	+5,796	−15,019
1989	−23,112	+1,481	−24,593	+2,261	−20,851
1990	−18,675	+1,518	−20,193	+4,295	−14,380
1991	−10,284	+1,208	−11,492	+3,657	−6,627
1992	−13,406	+1,487	−14,893	+4,069	−9,337

Sources   CSO, *United Kingdom Balance of Payments*, 1983, 1985, 1993, London; Business Briefing (1992), *Balance of Payments*, 29 May, British Chambers of Commerce, Chester.

facts: the increase in imports of finished goods; slower growth in exports because other countries during the latter part of the 1980s decade had lower growth rates; and the uncompetitive nature of UK exports due to a combination of qualitative difficulties, higher relative inflation in the UK and an over-priced currency buoyed up by high interest rates.

The Trading Patterns and Commodity Composition of the UK's Visible Trade

Table 4.2 shows an area analysis of UK visible trade and indicates a progressive move towards trade with Europe and the European Union (EU) in particular after 1973. Both the share of UK exports to and imports from Western Europe almost doubled during the period 1960–90 with the bias mainly towards the EU countries. The share of total visible trade with the US has remained steady, but has fallen with Canada. Similarly the trade with other Commonwealth countries such as Australia and New Zealand has fallen appreciably since 1969 due to the trade creation and deflection policies of being a member of the EU. The impact of oil on the the UK economy can be seen with the decline in imports from oil-exporting countries particularly after 1979.

The commodity composition of UK visible trade over the same period is shown in Table 4.3. If we take exports first, we can see that there has been a fall in the share of manufactured goods from 84 per cent in 1960 to 82 per cent in 1992; simultaneously there has been an increase in the share of oil-based products from 4 per cent to 6 per cent. On the imports side there has been a decline in the share of imports of food products, basic materials, and minerals and lubricants. This is not to say that the total amount of imports has not risen for these three categories, but that their share of total imports has declined. The impact of imports on the manufacturing sector makes interesting reading. The share of imports of manufactured goods out of total imports has risen from 33 per cent in 1960 to 79 per cent in 1992. In other words, import penetration in this sector has been so great that not only have imports of manufactures risen but also their proportion of total imports. In fact, the share of finished manufactured imports out of total imports has increased nearly fivefold. The table also indicates that the growth in imports of manufacturers was not in semi-manufactured goods since their share of total imports has only increased marginally. As we can see, therefore, the main problem for the UK was with finished manufactured goods.

The Trade in Manufactures

There have been major changes in the UK's export performance in and import penetration of manufactures. The UK's share of world trade in manufactures has declined from just over 25 per cent in 1950 to under 9 per cent by the early 1990s. The 30 years from 1950 to 1979 showed the greatest decline in manufacturing's share of world exports though there

TABLE 4.2
Area Composition of UK Visible Exports (X) and Imports (M) (% totals)

	1960		1969		1979		1989		1990		1992	
	X	M	X	M	X	M	X	M	X	M	X	M
1 Western Europe	32	31	40	38	57	60	59	65	62	65	64	65
(of which EEC)	(21)	(20)	(29)	(26)	(43)	(45)	(51)	(53)	(53)	(52)	(56)	(53)
2 North America	16	21	17	20	12	13	15	13	14	13	13	12
(of which USA)	(10)	(12)	(12)	(14)	(10)	(10)	(13)	(11)	(13)	(11)	(12)	(11)
3 Other developed countries	13	12	12	10	6	6	6	8	5	7	4	7
(of which Japan)	(1)	(1)	(2)	(1)	(2)	(3)	(2)	(6)	(3)	(5)	(2)	(6)
4 Oil-exporting countries	6	10	5	8	9	7	7	2	5	2	6	2
5 Other developing countries	31	23	23	20	13	11	11	10	12	11	12	12
6 Centrally planned economies	2	3	3	4	3	3	2	2	1	1	1	2

NOTE   Exports are measured free on board (f.o.b.), but imports include cost, insurance and freight (c.i.f.). All figures are rounded.

SOURCES   Central Statistical Office (1968, 1973, 1982, 1990) *Annual Abstract of Statistics*, CSO, London; Central Statistical Office (1993) *Monthly Digest of Statistics*, May, CSO, London.

TABLE 4.3
Commodity Composition of UK Visible Exports (X) and Imports (M) (% of total)

	1960		1969		1979		1989		1992	
	X	M	X	M	X	M	X	M	X	M
(0, 1)* Food beverages, tobacco	5	33	6	23	7	14	7	9	8	10
(2, 4) Basic materials	4	23	4	15	3	9	3	6	2	4
(3) Mineral fuel and lubricants	4	10	2	11	11	12	7	5	6	6
(5–8) Manufactured goods	84	33	85	50	76	63	81	79	82	79
(5, 6) (i) Semi-manufactured goods	(36)	(22)	(35)	(28)	(31)	(27)	(29)	(26)	(28)	(26)
(7, 8) (ii) Finished manufactured goods	(48)	(11)	(50)	(22)	(45)	(36)	(52)	(53)	(54)	(53)
(9) Unclassified	3	1	3	1	3	2	2	1	2	1

NOTES
Exports (f.o.b.), imports (c.i.f.). All figures are rounded.
* Numbers in brackets relate to the Standard International Trade Classification.
SOURCES   As for Table 4.2.

TABLE 4.4
Shares of World Trade in Manufactures (%)

	1950	1960	1970	1979	1990	1991
France	9.9	9.6	8.7	10.5	9.7	10
Germany	7.3	19.3	19.8	20.9	20.2	20
Japan	3.4	6.9	11.7	13.7	15.9	17
UK	25.5	16.5	10.8	9.1	8.6	9
USA	27.3	21.6	18.6	16.0	16.0	18

SOURCES   Brown, C.J.F. and Sheriff, T.D. (1979) 'De-Industrialisation: A Background Paper', in Blackaby, F. (ed.), *De-industrialisation*, London, Heinemann; Central Statistical Office (1991) *Monthly Review of External Trade Statistics*, London, HMSO; Organisation for Economic Co-operation and Development (OECD) (1992), *World Economic Outlook*, Paris, OECD

are indications that the UK's share during the 1980s has been bumping along the bottom. As Table 4.4 indicates, this decline in the share of world manufactures was not matched by any of the other major industrial countries and the most striking contrast over the last 30 years is that between the UK and Germany. In fact, while the volume of exports of manufactures from the developed economies grew by 48 per cent between 1980 and 1989, the volume of UK exports increased by only 30 per cent.

Looking at the other side of the market, that is imports, Table 4.5 leads us to believe that the UK economy faced increased competition from abroad leading to higher import penetration. Import penetration, that is the ratio of imports to total home demand for manufactured goods, has increased from 17 per cent in 1968 to 36 per cent in 1989. This level of import penetration has not been divided equally amongst all manufacturing sectors. It appears that those sectors which have been the back-bone of the UK's export performance in the past have been hit most heavily.

To some degree a level of import penetration would appear 'normal' since over time countries have tended to specialise in some and not all sectors of manufacturing; thus many other developed countries have also experienced import penetration in some commodity sectors. The degree to which this has happened in the UK is the main worry. Thus with import penetration rising and the world share of manufacturing declining it is not surprising that from 1983 onwards the UK has run a deficit on its manufactured trade account.

TABLE 4.5
Import Penetration in Manufactures for the UK (%)*

	1968	1973	1979	1989**
Total manufactures†	17	21	26	36
Vehicles	14	23	40	49
Electrical engineering	14	27	38	49
Mechanical engineering	20	26	32	41
Chemical and allied industries	18	22	30	41

NOTES
* Import penetration is defined as imports/home demand × 100.
** Series has been discontinued.
† Figures for total manufactures have been rounded off.
SOURCES Hewer, A. (1980) 'Manufacturing Industry in the Seventies:
An Assessment of Import Penetration and Export Performance',
Economic Trends, no. 370, June; Wells, J.D. and Imber, J.C. (1977)
'Home and Export Performance of United Kingdom Industries',
Economic Trends, no. 286, August; Central Statistical Office (1990)
United Kingdom Balance of Payments, CSO, London.

Factors Responsible for the Change in Export and Import Performance

A number of factors have been suggested to explain the deterioration in
the UK's trade performance in manufactures. It is possible that UK
exports are directed more to slower growing markets, though some studies
suggest that only one-third of the UK's slower export growth could be
attributed to trade with slower-growth economies. Moreover, since 1973
UK trade with Europe has grown rapidly and their economies cannot be
said to have had indifferent growth rates. It has been further suggested
that the UK could have had an inappropriate commodity composition –
once again this is unlikely to be the case since the commodity composition
of UK imports matches those of other industrialised countries – and that
the growth of UK export commodities was determined more by the growth
of world exports than by commodity composition. The OECD, on the
other hand, in comparing the growth of UK manufactured exports noted
the difference in both area and commodity composition of trade as a determinant of the UK's sluggish performance. However, they also stressed
other factors such as the effects of price and non-price competition

(OECD, source: OECD (1988/89), *The United Kingdom Economic Survey*, OECD, Paris).

The differences in the various elasticities of demand could be influential factors in the UK's trading performance. One estimate for the income elasticity of demand for UK exports is that it is less than 1 and much less favourable than that for Germany (2.5) and Japan (3.5). For total imports the UK income elasticity is estimated to be between 1.6 and 2, approximately in the ranges for the US and Germany, but for manufactured imports the UK income elasticity of demand is around 3. The implications we can draw from these figures is that when world income grows, UK imports, particularly of manufactured imports, rise faster than UK exports of manufactures and the balance of payments deteriorates. Moreover, there is a view that once imports of manufactures have increased they do not fall appreciably when the economy moves into recession – the so-called 'ratchet effect'.

Another important factor in describing the poor UK export performance is the tendency for firms to concentrate on the more secure home market when domestic demand is high. The reasons for this are fairly obvious: security, reduced language and cultural difficulties, reduced uncertainty of exchange rate variations and the like. Switching goods from export markets to domestic markets, however, reduces exports and satisfies demand at home in the short term only at the cost of important overseas markets in the long run.

It may also be that some firms have under-invested in the past and do not have the capacity to serve both domestic and foreign markets during boom periods. Therefore, during a boom not only do imports rise but exports are switched from the foreign to the domestic market. Investment takes time and given the poor track record of some UK firms in this area this pattern of behaviour is unlikely to alter in the future. Even those firms which surmount this problem tend to be those which are least open to foreign competition. It is also possible that an uneven amount of investment has gone into the service sectors, which are not so open to international trade. Thus the direction of investment may constrain the UK's ability to produce goods for world markets. An alternative argument is that the UK has never really faced a capacity constraint: it has simply faced higher import penetration than other countries. In fact, the problem for the UK may be one of better utilising existing capacity by making it more productive rather than increasing or raising capacity.

There are difficulties in measuring price competitiveness in the price elasticity of demand for exports, the ratio of UK export prices to a weighted average of competitors' prices or changes in costs. Putting these aside, however, there is little indication during the period 1975–90 that price factors were the dominant factor in contributing to the UK's export or import performance; non-price factors were seen to be of greater importance. So what are these non-price factors which appear to be of so much relevance?

Non-price Competitiveness

The non-price factors which may influence export and/or import performance include design, quality, maintenance, delivery date and after-sales service.

A 1981 report from the National Economic Development Office (NEDO) concluded that factors such as marketing and the presence or absence of non-tariff barriers were more influential for UK export sales than price variations. In addition, during the 1970s poor management and restrictive labour practices all combined to keep the quality of UK goods lower than other nations (NEDO, *Industrial Performance, Trade Performance and Marketing*, London: NEDO, 1981). The goal of reduced inflation during the 1980s may help the price competitiveness of UK exports but if non-price factors are more important then UK exports may continue to find it difficult in export markets. Moreover, in the area of sales and marketing it may be possible that the UK with its 'captive' Commonwealth market during the 1950s and 1960s did not need to market its products as actively, and thus its European neighbours and Japan in particular who were more active in other export markets stole a lead on the UK, a lead which the UK has found difficult to narrow.

In terms of product quality, high-priced products have usually embedded in them high levels of R&D, high levels of technology and a skilled workforce. It has been suggested that the UK is becoming biased towards low-quality products embodying older technology which tend to be lower-priced, whilst importing higher-quality products embodying a greater level of new technology. If the UK tends to export mainly mature products and import less-mature ones, then as a consequence it will suffer lower growth because the growth of sales in markets which are characterised by more mature products are slower on average than for new products. In addition, more mature products are open to greater competition from the Newly Industrialised Countries (NICs). During the latter part of the 1980s there were further indications that the UK was importing, in the area of machine tools, lower-quality imports which could have a major knock-on effect on the UK's ability to export high-quality products in the future. We should not deduce from these studies, however, that all sectors of the UK manufacturing industry were involved in low-quality exports and low-quality import substitutes (e.g. footwear). For example, in the chemical industry there has been a move from mass-produced chemical products towards the higher end of the market both in the UK and in Europe.

Returning to the area of income elasticities, if real incomes are growing over time and the UK is producing lower-quality products in some areas of manufacturing then it follows that in the long run UK products will be substituted for higher-quality products from other countries. In other words, the UK needs to be producing higher-technology products, otherwise its share of world exports will decline further and import penetration will continue to rise. There appears to be a strong relationship between technological competitiveness and trading performance; in other words, in those sectors where the UK produces highly technical/high-quality goods it is highly competitive and obtains a high level of exports in value terms. All is not lost, however, since there appeared to be a change in the income elasticity of demand for UK exports as the 1980s progressed. The rise, albeit a small one, may have been due to less-efficient firms leaving production, but it may also indicate that manufacturing firms were becoming more aware of the need to produce high-quality products. Even if this is the case, it could still be argued that the aggregate number of 'high-quality' firms in the UK is still too small due to the structural shake-out indicated in Chapter 2. One way forward for the UK is to improve the design and quality of its exports. This may require higher R&D expenditure, however: an area in which the UK has never been a market leader.

Why the Need for a Manufacturing Sector?

A number of factors have been suggested to explain why there has been a relative decline of the UK's manufacturing sector. Remedial action on some of these appears to be under way, but why do we need to worry when it has been argued that other sectors can take the place of manufacturing, particularly services, and that the process we are seeing is 'natural' for a maturing economy?

Even if we accept this argument, there are important features of the UK's trading performance that we should consider. The UK has one of the highest ratio of exports to GDP; thus if the growth in UK exports lags behind the growth in competitors' exports this has a greater impact on the UK economy. This is the balance of payments constraint on UK growth which forces the government to respond usually by raising interest rates and thereby attracting foreign capital into the country to balance the trading account. At the same time this imposes costs on UK industry leading to a downturn in investment either through the higher cost of borrowing, or through the downward revision of expectations, or through reduced consumer expenditure. For the UK around 40 per cent of all export earnings on the current account (visible and invisible) and about 40 per cent of all expenditure on imports derives from trade in manufactures. Thus if UK export markets are lost the current account runs into deficit. It is also true that the volume of UK exports has increased since 1980 in the region of some 30 per cent, but this is below the average for the EU and much less than the volume of import growth of manufactures into the UK. A UN report indicated within this context that the UK was the only major industrial country to experience a fall in its share of world manufactures and a rise in its share of total import of manufactures.

The direction of UK trade in manufactures is also changing. The UK trades more heavily with Europe (see Table 4.2), and it is these developed countries which are a greater threat to UK trade performance than LDCs or NICs. In other words, the argument that it is low-wage competition which is undermining the UK trading position is in some doubt. Moreover, given the growth of multinational companies, even when trade is taking place with a NIC it may well be with a multinational company whose home base is in a developed economy. Conversely, from a UK point of view the development of the Single European Market (SEM) has led to a disproportionate growth of non-European MNCs setting up in the UK. The success of these firms may alter the position of manufacturing in the UK's balance of payments and this we can already see with the export to Japan of Nissan cars made in Wearside, and the fact that the UK is now a net exporter of televisions, a commodity in which it does not have its own indigenous firm. Furthermore, it is suggested that by the middle of the 1990s the UK will once again become a net exporter of cars. Thus the manufacturing account could swing round in the UK's favour but ownership and control of the major manufacturing plants within the UK may be outside this country. In this scenario the possibility must always be there that a MNC may undergo restructuring, shifting its operating base from the UK to other sites in Europe, as Ford has done in the past, leaving behind unemployed factors of production, reducing the UK's export capacity and increasing imports.

If the manufacturing sector cannot grow quickly enough through either home or foreign investment, then one way out of the UK's problem on the external account is for the economy to grow at a slower rate than that of many of its major competitors. This would allow exports to rise, restrain imports and resolve the balance of payments constraint. Such a solution may be feasible on economic grounds but is unlikely to be acceptable politically. But if the UK cannot compete with its major competitors in the main industry markets this only leaves some high-quality niche markets or markets in low-wage/low-productivity/low-quality products in which the UK can operate.

Britain as a Low-wage, Low-productivity Economy

Productivity levels during the 1960s and 1970s were worse in the UK than in most other major industrial countries, and although the relative performance of the UK improved sharply in absolute terms during the 1980s productivity growth did not regain the level of the 1960s (see Table 4.6). There is no single conclusive determinant that has led to the UK's poor

TABLE 4.6
Productivity Growth in the Business Sector of OECD Countries
(% per year)

	Labour Productivity			Total Factor Productivity		
	1960–73	1973–9	1980–91	1960–73	1973–9	1980–91
Australia	3.2	2.0	1.2	2.9	1.2	0.7
Austria	5.8	3.3	1.9	3.4	1.4	0.8
Belgium	5.0	2.8	2.1	3.7	1.5	1.2
Canada	2.8	1.5	1.4	2.0	0.7	0.2
Denmark	4.3	2.6	2.3	2.8	1.2	1.4
Finland	5.0	3.4	3.3	3.4	1.7	2.0
France	5.4	3.0	2.4	3.9	1.7	1.5
Germany	4.6	3.4	1.8	2.7	2.0	1.2
Greece	8.8	3.4	1.0	5.8	1.5	0.6
Italy	6.3	3.0	1.8	4.6	2.2	1.1
Japan	9.4	3.2	2.9	6.4	1.8	1.9
Netherlands	4.9	3.3	1.4	3.1	2.0	0.9
New Zealand	1.8	–1.5	1.4	1.0	–2.2	0.4
Norway	4.1	0.1	1.1	3.6	–0.4	–0.1
Spain	6.1	3.8	2.6	4.2	1.7	1.8
Sweden	3.9	1.4	1.4	2.5	0.3	0.6
Switzerland	3.2	0.7	0.9	1.6	–0.9	0.3
UK	3.5	1.5	2.2	2.2	0.5	1.6
USA	2.8	0.6	1.0	1.8	0.1	0.5

SOURCE   Organisation for Economic Co-operation and Development (1993) *World Economic Outlook*, OECD, Paris.

productivity record but factors such as the lower levels of investment in manufacturing, inappropriate investment, overmanning, poor management and the use of ageing industrial equipment are all contributory factors.

Evidence from two NEDO surveys during the 1980s indicated that the returns to manufacturing investment during the period 1961–77 were 130 per cent greater in France, 81 per cent greater in West Germany and 32 per cent greater in the US compared with the UK. Their later study indicated that output per unit of net capital stock in manufacturing was 95 per cent higher in West Germany and 110 per cent higher in the US compared with the UK. (National Economic Development Office (NEDO) (1980, 1985) *British Industrial Performance*, London). One reason for the poor UK performance is the lower level of investment, but it is difficult to decide which factors are the dependent variables here; for example, low investment implies low productivity, which discourages investment in the UK. But even this circular argument is not as clear as it appears since a combination of factors could be in play, such as the poor choice of investment projects, less-effective and poorly trained management, a low-skilled workforce which through clinging to traditional working practices has not been as willing to take on new ideas and new methods of production. Lower educational attainment of all sectors of the workforce may be a key factor behind the UK's problems. Without higher skill levels workers may find it difficult to adapt to change and thus the lack of investment in physical and human capital may result in lower productivity and a lower quality of output.

To return once more to the topic of productivity: advances in this area observed in the UK during the 1980s may not be due to individuals working harder or to new capital equipment but simply to a reduction in overmanning, enabling a smaller workforce to produce the same output as before. None the less, it would be possible to be competitive in world markets if coupled with low productivity the UK had lower real wages. As Table 4.7 indicates, Germany has the highest hourly labour costs at $24. Switzerland is next at $22.5, with Belgium, France and Japan, following The UK is on $12. Thus on one level the UK is a relatively low-wage economy.

International competitiveness, in terms of unit labour costs, is also influenced by the exchange rate. If the exchange rate depreciates, in an economy where wages are rising faster than other countries' price competitiveness can be restored. In other words, lower relative unit labour costs could be achieved by reducing relative labour costs, by increasing productivity, by a depreciation in the currency, or by some combination of all three. All these factors appeared to move in the wrong direction in the UK between 1979 and 1981 resulting in a decline in output from the

TABLE 4.7
Hourly Wage Costs ($ 1993)

Country	Costs
Germany	23.8
Switzerland	22.5
Belgium	22.0
France	18.2
Japan	16.5
USA	15.5
UK	12.0
Hong Kong	5.6
China	0.6

SOURCE   *Lloyds Bank Economic Bulletin*, 'International Catch-up', no. 182, Feb. 1994.

manufacturing sector and a rise in unemployment. After 1981, the decline of sterling's effective exchange rate more than compensated for the rise in relative labour costs.

If we look at the consequences of a low-wage/low-productivity economy, we need to consider the role of technology. Technology tends to improve productivity, replacing labour which, because it is now in abundant supply, becomes the cheaper factor of production. In such a case firms may persist in using more labour-intensive techniques (unions may have a role to play here) even though new technology is available; thus lower quality products may be produced leading to a loss of market share. Such a process also encourages imports of better-quality goods. Moreover, the impact of lower real wages may have an important impact on overall consumer expenditure. If lower productivity, on the other hand, is not coupled with lower wages, MNCs may switch production to higher-productivity countries, leaving behind them lower output and unemployment. If on the other hand a country has a rise in labour costs relative to its main trading nations and it does not pass these on to the consumer in terms of higher prices, then profits will suffer. This downturn in profits leaves the firm open to takeover and reduces the funds available for investment. Without investment we may not be able to increase productivity and therefore profits. In addition, new technology is more easily accepted when output and productivity are rising and this stimulates further growth and productivity.

The consequences of low productivity and lack of competitiveness are easily seen in sectors which are involved more heavily in international trade, hence the preoccupation with the manufacturing sector. Within the context of some arguments here, we can see the predicament faced by the UK. Because of lower skill levels, lower relative investment and lower R&D, the UK may be becoming a lower-quality producer of manufactured goods in some sectors. These all help to explain why productivity levels are lower, and because skill levels are lower so average wages tend to be lower. Placing a greater emphasis on lower value-added products either through design or by force means that UK manufactured goods now face further competition from lower-wage producers in the LDCs and especially from the NICs. It would not appear that this pattern of production is sustainable in the long term.

The Costs of Growth

Growth brings benefits to an economy, as we have seen earlier, but corresponding to these benefits there are a number of potential costs. To achieve a higher growth rate some consumption may have to be forgone today and resources switched to investment so that future consumption may be higher. We illustrate this concept in Figure 4.1. The initial consumption level is shown as $C1$ and the growth path as $G1$. Suppose the government wishes to push the economy on to a higher growth path, shown as $G2$. To enable this growth path to be reached we require more investment, which could be financed through more savings or higher taxes, both of which reduce current consumption. As we can see, it takes until time Tx before the two growth paths coincide. Whether or not the sacrifice is worthwhile depends upon the amount of extra consumer goods produced in the future and how long it takes to make up for the sacrificed goods.

Growth itself may create extra demand; that is, the more you have the more you want. In this case the indifference curves of consumers move to the right faster than consumers' budget lines. In other words, as incomes grow the population may become more materialistic. As society proceeds along this path it is suggested that violence, crime and other social problems may increase.

Growth may cause negative externalities. As real national income grows it may impose costs on society in the form of pollution, noise and increased congestion. Many of these costs are likely to be understated since precise measurements are not available, but if the costs of growth were included in the estimates of real national income then the benefits of economic growth may be overstated.

FIGURE 4.1
Alternative Growth Paths

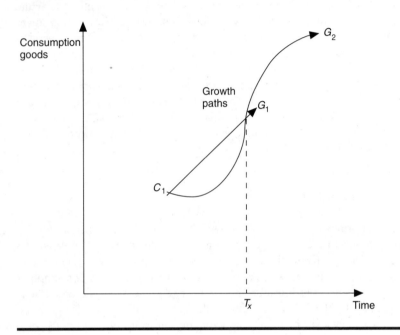

Growth also has an impact on resources, in particular on non-renewable ones. It is argued that because some resources are finite then some time in the future they must run out. If we increase our growth rate today we are just bringing the day forward when the non-renewable resources will disappear.

Growth also brings technical progress, which may create new jobs but at the same time may destroy others. Thus some people may find they have redundant skills; they may be forced to become unemployed or to take up low-paid, unskilled work.

Whether governments should pursue the goal of growth depends therefore on the costs and benefits of growth and how much weight individual groups in society attach to them. At the moment growth appears to be desirable, but perhaps a policy of constrained optimisation is a better path to follow. Here, growth is sought, but subject to levels of environmental protection, minimum wages, maximum rates of resource depletion, and so on.

The Limits to Growth

Growth may be constrained because of resource problems but also because an economy is not making the best use of its resources. We have seen that a point on the production possibility frontier indicates how resources can be combined to give the maximum potential output at any one time in an economy. It follows that when natural resources, labour or capital exist but go unused, potential output is lost. Hence any economic events that prevent the best use of resources limit the growth of the economy. The failure to employ resources fully is represented by any point inside the current production possibility curve. An economy that wishes to accelerate its output of consumption and capital goods could be limited in its efforts by decisions that result in unemployment of resources. For example, the use of monetary and fiscal policy to achieve price stability may restrict total expenditure in an economy and unemployment is a common result. In other words because there are conflicting economic goals this may limit the achievement of growth.

The other aspect of the limits to growth argument is that couched in the cost of growth. Although the level of growth is seen as an indication of the wellbeing of an economy, recently questions have been raised as to whether continued economic growth is possible given the physical constraints of our planet: do the costs of growth outweigh the benefits from growth?

If growth proceeds exponentially and resources are finite some time in the future there will be point where all these resources are used up and economic growth will grind to a halt. The catastrophe, if it comes, will be fairly sudden and even if we realise it is coming our behaviour will be such that we cannot change our ways quick enough. The problem is seen from a number of perspectives: the depletion of resources, the continued rise in population, and the problem of pollution. Such ideas are not new. We only have to look at Malthus' theory of population to see an earlier forerunner.

Critics suggest that the price mechanism will prevent such a scenario occurring. In their view, as a resource is depleted so the price will rise and we will consume less of it. At the same time, however, we will switch demand to a suitable substitute good. As we do so the price of these substitute goods will rise. It is also possible that resources which were not profitable to use at the old price levels will now come into use. These marginal resources may be used effectively and efficiently if technology can provide a means of increasing the capacity usage. Thus technology enables us to obtain from marginal resources a level of output which keeps consumers 'happy'.

Suppose, however, that there comes a point when technology cannot make marginal resources as effective as those that have been depleted. It follows that the prices of materials would rise; this would feed through to inflation, and a wage price spiral would ensue, making everyone's standard of living decline. Alternatively resources could be rationed, but once again living standards would decline. Given this latter scenario, perhaps governments should not be striving for all-out growth but for a satisfactory level of growth subject to resource depletion. This argument, even as improbable as some see it, received further support at the Earth summit in Rio de Janeiro in May 1992. The call was for sustainable development if the gap between poor and rich countries was to be bridged. However, although the rich countries seem most concerned about negative externalities, it is these same countries which consume around 70 per cent of all resources, produce the greatest amount of pollution and 45 per cent of greenhouse gases.

The Social Limits to Growth

We have seen that an increase in GNP or GDP is synonymous with growth and have stated the limits to growth argument. There is, however, another feature to consider in the growth process: is a country's GNP related to an improvement in its citizens' standard of living?

There are two issues here; one is that it is possible that goods and services are produced that give short-term pleasure rather than long-term satisfaction; secondly, can society's 'happiness' or wellbeing be increased through the process of growth? If it cannot, is growth self-defeating? As societies grow and individuals purchase commodities in excess of their basic needs, the satisfaction that individuals derive from consumption depends not only on their own consumption levels but on the consumption levels of others as well. For example, the satisfaction derived from owning a radio depends to a large extent on the number of people owning radios, since scarcity is reduced and there is an increase in the noise factor. In other words, people like to own goods others cannot have; once others do have them the satisfaction from owning them is reduced. Thus if economic growth enables individuals to have more of a good the satisfaction or wellbeing of the individual depends not only on his own consumption but on the consumption levels of others as well.

It also appears that certain goods and facilities from which individuals derive satisfaction are subject to absolute limitations in supply. Such goods are called positional goods, whose availability is fixed, either because of physical scarcity or because of social scarcity. It is interesting to contrast positional goods and material goods. The supply of material goods is not fixed but increases in line with output per head. The value of positional goods, for example, a country cottage, derives from the element of scarcity embodied in them. As an economy grows and material goods increase along with it, then they will be less highly valued than positional goods whose supply cannot be increased. In other words, the items which are valued the most are those goods that economic growth in the current time period cannot provide.

This concept of positional and material goods is also related to public and private goods. A pure public good is one that is non-excludable and non-rival, such as defence; and a pure private good is both rival and excludable, for example, food. A great many goods are neither pure public goods nor pure private goods since they possess the elements of rivalry or non-excludability, depending upon the conditions of use. For example, a public park may be non-excludable but it becomes a rival good when over-crowding occurs; in other words, when externalities exist. This feature of externality is a problem with growth and it is clear that economic growth which increases everybody's income does not reduce the extent of these negative externalities. Thus it follows that there is an increased role for state intervention as economies grow, though there is the converse argument that state intervention leads to inefficiencies. If one country intervenes to reduce the externalities that exist through growth it may penalise its own industries thereby making them less competitive, reducing productivity and increasing costs. In such a situation one country alone may not intervene and it will require intervention on a gloal scale to reduce world externalities.

Can Britain Escape Slow Growth?

The growth rates recorded by most economies during the early part of the 1990s have been poor, for example OECD economic growth virtually stopped in the first half of 1991. However, a return by some countries to positive growth rates was seen in 1992 and 1993 but these were very sluggish. None the less, when positive growth rates do return there is expected to be a general convergence of growth and inflation performance in the major industrial economies. From the point of view of inflation, convergence will help UK exports, which will become more price-competitive. However, we have seen that other non-price factors are important in establishing Britain's export performance. We have seen also that although productivity in the UK during some years in the 1980s exceeded that of our European competitors, when averaged out over the whole decade it was no more than a return to the trend experienced in the early 1970s, so Britain's productivity has not been kicked permanently on to a higher plane. In addition, although the UK is catching up its major competitors within Europe, the difference between UK and US productivity rates does not seem to be narrowing. We have also seen the relevance of the balance of payment constraint for the UK economy and its influence on the UK's growth record. The deficit on the current account has been much reduced in the early 1990s from the level of over £20 billion in 1989, but this has been at a cost of rising unemployment and slower growth. Once the economy comes out of recession the forecasts are for the trade deficit to widen once more, which will again need financing. Such a process may lead to an upward pressure on interest rates in the UK relative to other members in the OECD. The rise in interest rates will bring the cycle around once more: investment will be reduced and confidence dented, both of which will constrain growth. Over the remaining part of the decade there are also important external forces in play. The SEM will reduce barriers within EU countries, the result of which may lead to increased pressure on the UK's manufacturing sector, especially as we have seen that the developed economies of Europe reaped most of the benefit from the UK's deindustrialisation.

It is suggested that if Britain is to escape the problem of slow growth a combined industrial and trade strategy is required. Given the decline in the manufacturing sector and the resultant displacement of manufacturing towards many low value-added markets, there is a need to concentrate on investment in technologically progressive industries, coupled with skill and educational training so that British industry produces the items demanded both by British consumers and by world markets. It may also be possible for the UK to indulge in trade policies to promote exports and deflect imports which do not violate Britain's membership of the EU and the GATT. Even if Britain does nothing the EU may be reconciled to undertaking a much more overt industrial policy, since without it convergence of the major industrial countries may not be a possibility, and such convergence is needed in order to develop a single currency within Europe.

Could the UK learn from from successful countries such as Japan and Germany to improve her growth rate? There are obvious changes that have been made within the UK economy, such as the development of single-union agreements, greater attention to the supply chain, changes in production methods such as 'just in time' management and 'total quality management', greater involvement of workers and management in decision-making, and the development of closer relationships with banks modelled on the *Hausbank* procedure used in Germany.

Not all differences between Germany and Japan and the UK have been introduced here satisfactorily. Changes in working practices have been one success story, and the productivity of Japanese companies in the UK matches or exceeds those of similar plants in other areas of Europe. None the less, the Japanese have been reluctant to bring their R&D plants to external markets; one reason is that there are not sufficient high-quality engineers in the UK to justify locating their R&D departments here. Furthermore, Japanese-owned companies (and to some extent privately owned companies, such as JCB) appear to be much more successful at implementing Japanese-style management practices than are publicly owned British companies. Thus until the publicly owned sector changes, the upturn in British industry will be limited. In addition, there is a need for UK companies to build long-term relationships between suppliers, employees and customers.

On a macroeconomic level, the German and Japanese economies have a far better record on inflation. This has tended to be lower in these countries and far less variable than in the UK. At least some part of the lower cost of capital in Germany and Japan has been linked to the relative stability of inflation. The areas of skill-training, education or vocational training are also important features in which Britain should invest more heavily. Furthermore, the level of competition is important in the structure, conduct and performance of industry. There is a high level of competition in both Japan and Germany in each of the sectors in which their industries excel. Thus by providing a more competitive environment UK firms may enhance their productivity. The SEM may provide this on a European level, though national governments still persist in the idea of 'European national champions'. Finally, we must remember that what works in Germany and Japan may not work in the UK, nor may we wish to use some of their procedures and practices. None the less, there are lessons to be learnt from successful countries.

The UK's Attempts to Stimulate Growth

It is unlikely that the UK has opted for slower growth than its major competitors. In its attempt, however, to emulate other countries there have been a whole range of circumstances which various governments in the UK might say have militated against the UK being a high-productivity/high-growth economy. The 1980s have certainly seen a shake-up in the structure of British industry, and the changes that have taken place here are surely not at an end. UK industry may be leaner and fitter but, as the argument goes, there may not be enough of it.

Macroeconomic policies which endeavour to create growth now serve to drag in imports since UK industry is not large enough and does not provide some of the goods required by British consumers or industry. Furthermore, it is hard to concur that supply-side policies have worked to reduce the balance of payments constraint since a decade of such policies have left the UK's balance of payments in a still far from healthy position. Neither can we rely on a depreciation of the exchange rate to restore the UK's competitiveness since this process increases inflationary pressures. One estimate was that a growth rate of only 0.9 per cent per year with a fixed or managed exchange rate was possible if the UK did not wish to incur balance of payments problems. If we reject the balance of payments constrained growth rate theory then it implies acceptance of the classical orthodoxy that economies tend to full employment notwithstanding the condition of their balance of payments.

However, should we really be going for growth at a time when the world is becoming increasingly concerned about global warming and the depletion of finite resources? A rate of growth constrained by the level of finite resources – a sustainable level of growth – may be easier to bear for developed countries, but for many LDCs or NICs the development of indigenous natural resources is seen as a prerequisite for escape from low levels of GDP per capita. Thus they appear to accept this scenario only if the developed nations provide increased aid to finance any difference between sustainable growth and their normal level of growth.

But where does this leave the UK? Putting aside the world-wide problems of growth, the UK must seek some means by which its growth rate can be kicked onto a higher level, and the succeeding chapters indicate how this can be achieved. If the UK does nothing it may have to face the fact that it will continue to be a low-growth economy and suffer the consequences thereof.

Explaining Economic Growth 5

Ascertaining the factors that are specifically related to the poor growth record of the UK are difficult; none the less, the problems being faced by the British economy can be clearly seen in Table 5.1. Britain's growth rate has been lagging behind that of its major competitors for well over a century. Economic theory in general provides important insights into the reasons why some countries have proved so much more successful than others. And, however elegant, economic growth theories all start from a recognition that there are certain key sources of economic growth.

TABLE 5.1
Average Annual Growth Rates, 1870–1992

	1870–1913	1913–50	1950–73	1973–92
Britain	1.9	1.3	3.0	1.6
France	1.5	1.1	5.0	2.2
Germany	2.8	1.3	5.9	2.3
Italy	1.9	1.5	5.6	2.9
Japan	2.3	2.2	9.3	3.9
United States	3.9	2.8	3.6	2.4

SOURCES   Maddison, A. (1991) *Dynamic Forces in Capitalist Development* (London: Oxford University Press); *Lloyds Bank Economic Bulletin*, 'The Economic Outlook', no. 166, Oct 1992.

The Aggregate Production Function

Common sense suggests that, for a given stock of natural resources, there are three main sources of economic growth: technological progress, increases in the capital stock and increases in labour input. For example, the rise in per capita output over the post-war period clearly reflects advances in knowledge: notably, the advent of cheap, powerful computers, the harnessing of nuclear power, and developments in telecommunications. But it also stems from investment in new and more efficient plant and equipment and in new motorways, airports and other physical infrastructure, as well as the creation of a better-educated labour force capable of using the new technologies.

The basic relationship between growth, technological progress, capital and labour is captured in the so-called 'aggregate production function' (APF), sometimes called the Cobb–Douglas production function. The aggregate production function can be expressed in simplified form as follows:

$$Y = AK^\alpha L^\beta$$

where Y is output, A represents the state of technology, K is the capital stock, α is the capital elasticity of output, L is the labour stock (number of person-hours) and β is the labour elasticity of output. (A more detailed explanation is given in Appendix 2 to this chapter.) The capital elasticity of output measures the impact on output of a given increase in the capital stock. For example, with α equal to 0.8, a 10 per cent increase in the capital stock would, *ceteris paribus*, lead to an 8 per cent (0.8 × 10 per cent) increase in output. Similarly, with a labour elasticity of output of 0.4, a 10 per cent increase in labour input would lead to a 4 per cent increase in output.

The law of diminishing returns suggests that α and β should both be less than unity; that is, with other factors fixed, increases in capital (or labour) add less than proportionately to output so long as the other factor of production is fixed. If both factors are increased together, the value of $\alpha + \beta$ reflects the impact of scale on output. For example, if $\alpha + \beta = 1.2$, then a balanced 10 per cent increase in both capital and labour will increase output by 12 per cent (that is, the 10 per cent increase in capital contributes 8 per cent, the 10 per cent increase in labour adds 4 per cent). In other words, if $\alpha + \beta$ exceeds unity, the aggregate production function is said to exhibit increasing returns to scale, and vice versa (see Table 5.2).

Table 5.3 provides empirical estimates (from the famous Moroney study in the late 1960s) of the sizes of the output elasticities of capital and labour

TABLE 5.2
The Aggregate Production Function

Values of α, β	Properties of the Aggregate Production Function
$\alpha, \beta < 1$	Decreasing marginal productivity
$\alpha, \beta = 1$	Constant marginal productivity
$\alpha, \beta > 1$	Increasing marginal productivity
$\alpha + \beta < 1$	Decreasing returns to scale
$\alpha + \beta = 1$	Constant returns to scale
$\alpha + \beta > 1$	Increasing returns to scale

TABLE 5.3
Estimated Output Elasticities for Selected Industries

Industry	Output Elasticity of Capital (α)	Output Elasticity of Labour (β)
Chemicals	0.20	0.89
Printing	0.46	0.62
Electrical Machinery	0.37	0.66
Textiles	0.12	0.88
Petroleum	0.31	0.64

SOURCE Moroney, J. (1967) 'Cobb–Douglas Production Functions and Returns to Scale in the United States', *Western Economic Journal*.

for a range of industries. It confirms that, in line with economic theory, these elasticities are less than unity (that is, the law of diminishing returns applies) and, more significantly, that constant returns to scale appear, broadly speaking, to be the norm.

Table 5.4 shows the annual average growth rates of the productive capital stock in the main industrialised countries. It shows that, while investment in new plant and equipment has slowed in all five countries since 1973, Britain still continues to lag behind its international competitors.

Table 5.5 examines the contribution of labour input over the last decade. In Britain, as elsewhere, employment has generally grown slowly over time. A key influence on employment has been population growth,

TABLE 5.4
Annual Average Growth of Productive Capital Stock (per cent)

Country	1950–73	1973–87
Britain	5.7	2.3
France	6.4	3.7
Germany	7.7	2.7
Japan	10.2	6.7
United States	3.8	2.6

SOURCE   OECD (1988) *World Economic Outlook*, OECD, Paris.

which has averaged around 0.4 per cent per annum in Britain since 1900. At the same time, there have been conflicting social and demographic factors which have complicated the relationship between population and employment growth. Life expectancy has been steadily improving, increasing the proportion of the population who are retired; taken together with earlier retirement and the secular increase in the period spent in full-time study by the young, this has reduced the rate of employment growth associated with any given rate of population growth. On the other hand, there has been a sharp rise in female participation rates, with more married woman going out to work. On balance, these effects have tended to neutralise each other, so that employment growth has broadly mirrored population trends.

However, labour input is the product of total employment and the average number of hours worked. And while employment has been growing slowly, employees have typically been working fewer hours per week and for fewer weeks per year. Table 5.5 shows that, in fact, in all the

TABLE 5.5
Annual Average Growth of Labour Input, 1900–87 (per cent)

Country	Employment	Hours Worked	Labour input
Britain	0.5	–0.7	–0.2
France	0.1	–0.7	–0.6
Germany	0.7	–0.6	0.1
Japan	1.0	–0.3	0.7
United States	1.6	–0.6	1.0

SOURCE   Maddison, op. cit. (Table 5.1).

major economies the average number of hours worked per person has declined. For Britain, in particular, this latter effect swamped the impact of growing employment, so that overall labour input actually declined at an average rate of 0.2 per cent per annum.

Total Factor Productivity

The Nobel Prize winner Robert Solow laid many of the foundations of modern economic growth theory during the 1950s. One of his many contributions was to point out that, by calculating the impact on growth of observed changes in capital and labour inputs, that part of economic growth which remained 'unexplained' must be due to technological progress. In other words, the effect of technological progress (which causes an increase in 'total factor productivity') can be estimated as the residual between total economic growth and that part which is explained by increases in capital and labour inputs. Solow's famous 'decomposition' states that:

$$g = \frac{\delta A}{A} + \alpha \frac{\delta K}{K} + (1 - \alpha) \frac{\delta L}{L}$$

where g is the growth rate and δ denotes 'change in'. Technological progress, or total factor productivity is captured by the term $\frac{\delta K}{K}$, while the rate of capital accumulation, $\frac{\delta A}{A}$, contributes to growth in proportion to capital's share of output, α. Similarly, the rate of increase of labour input adds to growth in proportion to labour's share of output, $(1-\alpha)$. Rearranging the Solow decomposition yields:

$$\frac{\delta A}{A} = \alpha(g - \frac{\delta K}{K}) + (1 - \alpha)(g - \frac{\delta L}{L})$$

where all the variables on the right-hand side of the equation are observable. It is therefore a relatively straightforward exercise to calculate the value of the residual, $\frac{\delta A}{A}$. Table 5.6 shows one estimate of the size of this residual, total factor productivity. It shows that between one-third and one-half of economic growth is due to technological progress, rather than increases in capital and labour inputs.

TABLE 5.6
The Solow Decomposition: Average Annual Growth Rates, 1900–87

Country	Output	Contribution of Capital and Labour	Residual
Britain	2.0	1.2	0.8
France	2.8	1.2	1.6
Germany	3.0	1.4	1.6
Japan	5.1	3.3	1.8
United States	3.0	2.2	0.8

SOURCE   Maddison, op. cit. (Table 5.1).

Table 5.7 shows the growth of total factor productivity over the post-war period for Britain and its main international competitors. It highlights the so-called 'productivity slowdown', which appears to have taken place after the first oil price shock in 1973. The rate of technological innovation clearly depends upon research and development (see Chapter 8). Traditional theories of economic growth typically treat technological progress as exogenous, although economists increasingly recognise that the pace of investment and innovation (that is, the commercial exploitation of inventions) depends upon macroeconomic conditions; for example, the rate of economic growth, the structure of taxes, patent legislation, and so on.

TABLE 5.7
Total Factor Productivity: Annual Average Growth Rates (%)

Country	1950–73	1973–87
Britain	0.7	0.7
France	1.8	0.6
Germany	2.1	0.5
Japan	1.2	0.2
United States	0.8	0.1

SOURCE   Maddison op. cit. (Table 5.1).

Economic Growth in the Aggregate Supply and Demand Model

These concepts can be easily fitted into the simple aggregate supply and demand model (see Figure 5.1). The aggregate supply schedule (*AS*) shows how much firms in the economy will produce at different price levels (P), while the aggregate demand schedule (AD) shows the quantities of output (Y) that the nation as a whole (households, businesses and government taken together) want to buy at different price levels. From year to year, aggregate demand fluctuates, often causing quite sharp changes in output (Y) which are independent of developments on the supply side. But, in the long run, it is the more fundamental changes on the supply side of the economy, namely, technological progress and increases in capital and labour, that allow economies to enjoy ever-higher levels of output. Within the context of the aggregate supply and demand model, underlying improvements in the supply side manifest themselves as a continuous, rightward shift in the aggregate supply schedule over time (for example, from AS_0 to AS_1 to AS_2), steadily increasing the quantity of output that firms supply at any given level of aggregate demand from Y_0 to Y_1 to Y_2 (see Figure 5.1).

FIGURE 5.1
Aggregate Demand, Aggregate Supply Model

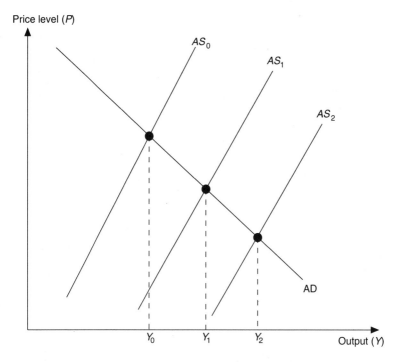

To understand the reasons for rightwards shifts in the aggregate supply schedule, the obvious starting point is to consider the relationship between the aggregate supply schedule and the aggregate production function. In the short run, it is assumed that all factors of production except labour are fixed; specifically, it is assumed that there is a given state of technology and a fixed capital stock. On this basis, the aggregate production function (APF) shown in Figure 5.2 can be drawn. It shows that the law of diminishing returns applies (that is, the labour elasticity of output is less than unity). With all other factors of production fixed, as firms employ more and more labour, output rises, but at a diminishing rate; that is, as firms expand employment, the marginal product of labour decreases.

FIGURE 5.2
The Aggregate Production Function

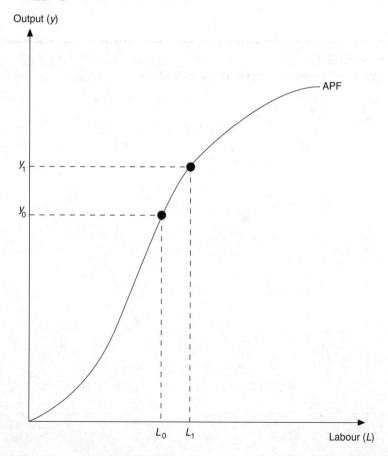

The Role of the Labour Market

How much labour will it be profitable for all firms to employ? To answer this question, it is necessary to move to the labour market itself. Basic microeconomics teaches that profit-maximising firms hire labour up to the point where the last worker adds as much to total costs (that is, the wage paid) as he or she adds to the firm's total revenue. The extra revenue generated is known as the 'marginal revenue product' (MRP). Assuming perfectly competitive goods markets, the marginal revenue product is simply the price of the product multiplied by marginal product (the increase to output contributed by the last worker). Implicit in the shape of the aggregate production function is the assumption that marginal product declines as employment increases. Figure 5.3 shows that for a given set of product prices (that is, a given price level, P_0), the demand for labour schedule is simply the downward-sloping marginal revenue product schedule for the economy as a whole, $MRP(P_0)$. It shows that, with the price level given, as the (money) wage rate falls, firms in aggregate will find it profitable to employ more workers. What about the supply of labour? All other things equal, at any given price level the higher the wage, the greater the amount of labour offered. For a price level P_0, the labour supply schedule is upward-sloping at $L_s(P_0)$.

Assuming that the labour market is perfectly competitive, employment and wages will be determined in the normal way by the intersection of the labour supply and demand schedules. In other words, for a given set of product prices, a fixed stock of land and capital and labour's relative preferences for work *vis-à-vis* leisure (which determine the shape and position of the labour supply schedule), the equilibrium wage rate, W_0, and level of employment, L_0, can be worked out. Moreover, by going back to the aggregate production function in Figure 5.2, the level of output, Y_0, consistent with equilibrium in the labour market can be read off.

The Short-run Aggregate Supply Schedule

To derive the aggregate supply schedule, it is necessary to examine what happens to employment and output if prices in the economy rise. Suppose that prices rise from the original price level, P_0, to P_1. How does this affect the labour market presented in Figure 5.4? Consider first the situation of firms when the price level changes. Firms maximise profit by altering employment until the money wage is equal to marginal revenue product. Each firm in turn calculates its marginal revenue product by referring to the price of its own product, which it knows day by day. Thus, a 10 per

FIGURE 5.3
Equilibrium in the Labour Market

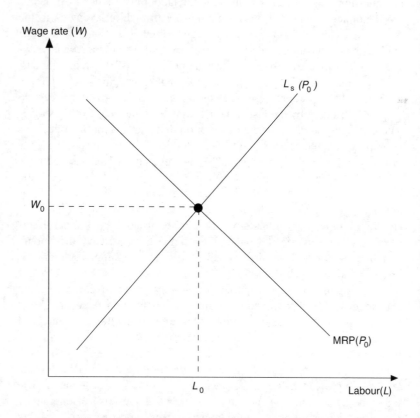

cent rise in the price level, which increases all individual product prices by 10 per cent, increases each firm's marginal revenue product at any given level of employment by 10 per cent. Each firm can see the increase as soon as it takes place and adjusts its level of employment immediately. When the price level increases from P_0 to P_1, the demand for labour schedule in Figure 5.4 thus shifts to the right from $MRP(P_0)$ to $MRP(P_1)$.

Now consider the situation from the point of view of individual workers. The labour supply schedule (in terms of money wages) depends on the price level. All other things being equal, a 10 per cent rise in prices will cause workers to require 10 per cent higher money wages for any given number of hours' work. But the price with which workers are con-

FIGURE 5.4
Labour Market Equilibrium and Money Illusion

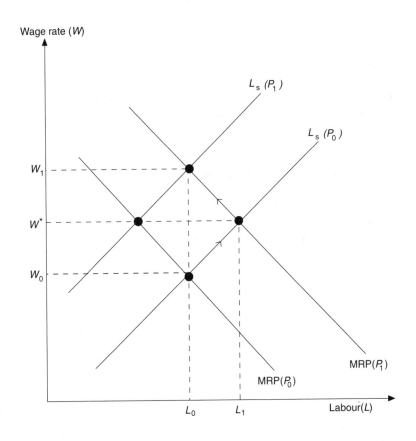

cerned is not the price of an individual product, but the price of all goods and services in the economy. This information is only available with a time lag and, as some prices (such as those for fruit and vegetables) fluctuate month by month due to seasonal effects, it may take some time before a clear change in average prices becomes apparent.

What this means is that while firms respond instantaneously to a change in average prices, it may be some time before workers fully appreciate what has happened to the price level. In the intervening period, they suffer 'money illusion', unable to appreciate that the value of money has changed and accordingly selling their labour at too high or too low a money wage. In Figure 5.4, because workers fail to appreciate that prices have risen in the short run, they supply exactly the same amount of labour as before at any given money wage; that is, the labour supply schedule remains at $L_s(P_0)$. The result is that, as long as money illusion persists, the effect of the rise in prices is to shift the demand for labour to the right from $MRP(P_0)$ to $MRP(P_1)$, while leaving the supply of labour unchanged at $L_s(P_0)$. Employment increases and, by checking with the aggregate production function in Figure 5.2, it can be seen that the effect of the price rise is to increase output to Y_1. In the short run, therefore, while money illusion persists, workers are effectively tricked into working harder for lower 'real wages' (NB: the real wage at L_1 is $W*/P_1$, which is lower than W_0/P_0). The aggregate supply is upward-sloping (see Figure 5.5). When prices rise from P_0 to P_1, output increases from Y_0 to Y_1.

FIGURE 5.5
The Aggregate Supply Curve in the Short-run

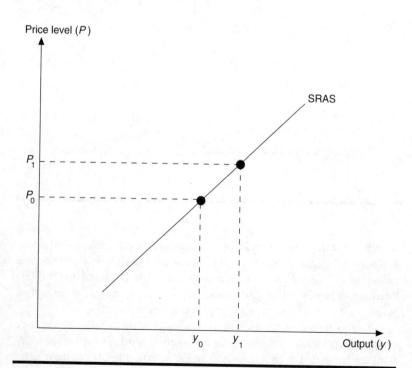

The Long-run Aggregate Supply Schedule

Gradually, however, workers come to realise that prices have changed, reducing the purchasing power of the wages they receive. For this reason, the aggregate supply schedule in Figure 5.5 is labelled the 'short-run aggregate supply' (SRAS) schedule, to signify that it exists only in the short run. In the long run, the labour supply schedule moves to the left from $L_s(P_0)$ to $L_s(P_1)$, as workers demand compensating wage increases (see Figure 5.4). Eventually money wages rise by the full amount of the price increase (rising further from W^* to W_1), real wages return to their earlier level (i.e., $W_1/P_1 = W_0/P_0$) and the economy returns to Y_0. In other words, in the long run the economy always comes back to Y_0 and an increase in the price level from P_0 to P_1 will simply increase money wages from W_0 to W_1, without having any effect on either output, employment or real wages. The long-run aggregate supply schedule (LRAS) is vertical at Y_0 (see Figure 5.6), where Y_0 is the 'natural rate of output' – that is, the rate of output consistent with long-run equilibrium in the labour market. The short-run aggregate supply schedule, SRAS(P_0), only exists for the period during which labour supply decisions are being made on the basis of an expected price level, P_0; as workers' expectations adjust and feed through into higher wages at every level of employment, so the short-run supply schedule gradually shifts left, eventually stabilising at SRAS(P_1), where the actual and expected price level are once again the same.

Economic Growth and Long-run Aggregate Supply

Economic growth can thus be represented in the aggregate supply and demand model as a rightwards shift in the long-run aggregate supply schedule – for example, from LRAS$_0$ to LRAS$_1$ in Figure 5.7a. At LRAS$_1$, the economy can enjoy more goods and services at any given price level (i.e., Y_1 rather than Y_0). How could such an increase in the underlying or long-run level of output come about? First, consider the labour market in Figure 5.7c. If the labour supply were to increase – either because there was an increase in the number of workers available for employment or because the existing workforce became prepared to offer more hours' labour at any given money wage – this would shift the labour supply schedule to the right from L_{s0} to L_{s1} (at any given price level), raising equilibrium employment from L_0 to L_1. The rate of output consistent with the equilibrium in the labour market would accordingly increase from Y_0 to Y_1 for a given production function, APF$_0$ (see Figure 5.7b), shifting the long-run aggregate supply schedule from LRAS$_0$ to LRAS$_1$ in Figure 5.7a.

FIGURE 5.6
The Aggregate Supply Curve in the Long-run

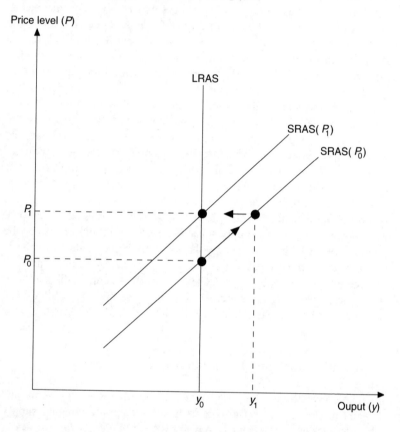

Secondly, look at Figure 5.7b. If the short-run aggregate production function were to shift upwards from APF_0 to APF_1, this would mean that at every level of employment, a greater amount of output can be produced than before (NB: any change in the aggregate production function will also affect the marginal revenue product of labour, but this complication is ignored here for simplicity of exposition). With equilibrium employment unchanged at L_0, the level of output would increase, as before, from Y_0 to Y_1. The short-run aggregate production function could shift upwards if:

FIGURE 5.7
The Impact of Economic growth on Output, Employment and the Wage Rate

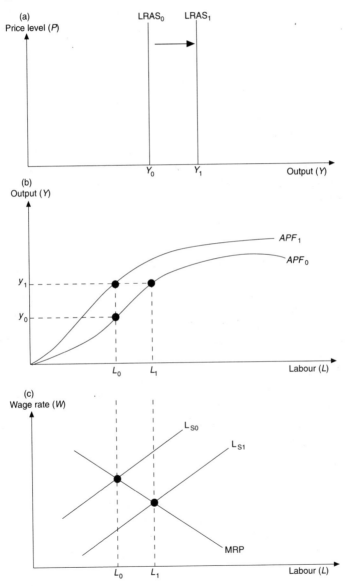

1. the productivity of labour were to rise, because the 'quality' of labour was increased through better training and education;
2. the capital stock were to rise, allowing each employee to produce more output for a given number of hours worked; or
3. technological progress were to improve the 'quality' of the capital stock, enabling each worker to produce more output from a given amount of machinery.

To summarise, the natural rate of output will increase (that is, the long-run aggregate supply schedule will shift to the right) if the labour supply schedule shifts to the right or if the aggregate production function shifts upwards; that is, if the labour input increases or if there is either technological progress or an increase in the capital stock. As noted above, for the British economy, where reductions in average hours worked have tended to outweigh increases in the numbers in employment, the former route holds out little promise for sustained economic growth. On the other hand, technological progress and capital investment are the key to long-term economic success.

Underlying Factors and Stimuli for Growth

Numerous factors have been suggested as to what might be the underlying determinants of economic growth. The discussion here has led to a broad conclusion that technological progress, capital investment and labour input are the major determinants of the growth process. For Britain and the other major industrial economies technological progress and capital investment each account for approximately half of observed economic growth, with the trend to fewer working hours typically cancelling out any potential contribution from increasing employment.

This chapter has also synthesised these insights from economic growth theory with the standard, static aggregate supply and demand model. In terms of the aggregate supply and demand model, economic growth constitutes a rightwards shift in the long-run aggregate supply schedule and that this effect can be produced by either an increase in the supply of labour (which raises equilibrium employment/labour input) or by technological progress or capital investment, which works by shifting the short-run aggregate production function upwards.

The question that has been left unanswered is which factors influence each of these driving forces that underpin economic growth? How does the tax and social security system affect the labour supply? Is the best way of stimulating private-sector investment in human and physical capital an unregulated, *laissez faire* environment? Or is activist demand management necessary to guarantee firms a healthy, growing market for output, thereby encouraging investment and risk-taking? What is the role for fiscal incentives (for example, tax allowances, public subsidies) to promote investment and R&D? Economists have produced no clear-cut answers to these critical questions. Chapters 6 and 7 explore the basic theoretical differences between the Keynesians, who argue that government intervention is necessary for a strong supply side, and the New Classical school which argues for a deregulated, liberalised economy in which the free market can operate unhindered.

Appendix 1: Economic Growth and the Business Cycle

The aggregate supply and demand model used above is a 'static equilibrium model'; that is, it attempts to explain the equilibrium *levels* of output and prices under a given set of circumstances. Such static equilibrium models are very useful for analysing the fundamental reasons for changes in the economy. But, in the real world, economists are typically more concerned with 'dynamic' scenarios; that is, we are more interested in explaining changes in the rate of growth of output rather than the absolute level, or changes in the inflation rate rather than the absolute price level. The simple, static aggregate supply and demand model can, however, be transformed into a dynamic model relatively easily. The formal derivations of the aggregate supply and aggregate demand schedules are more complex, but the model itself is intuitively straightforward to understand, sharing many of the properties of its static equivalent. In what follows, the derivation of the schedules is not considered in depth, but the basic dynamic model is presented and used to show how economic growth varies throughout the course of a typical business cycle.

The essential difference between the static and dynamic aggregate supply and demand models is that in the latter the axes relate to rates of change – that is, the rate of (price) inflation, $\dot{P}$, rather than the price level, P, and the rate of economic growth, $\dot{Y}$ rather than the level of output, Y (NB: the dot above the variables denotes 'rate of change in'). Consider first the long-run growth (LRG) schedule in Figure 5.8. In this dynamic version, the long-run trend, or natural, rate of economic growth, $\dot{Y}_N$, can be drawn in, which is the rate of growth given the underlying rate of technological progress, capital accumulation (physical and human) and labour input. This equilibrium rate of growth is independent of the rate of inflation and the long-run growth schedule is therefore vertical.

FIGURE 5.8
Equilibrium Growth in a Dynamic Aggregate Demand, Aggregate Supply Model

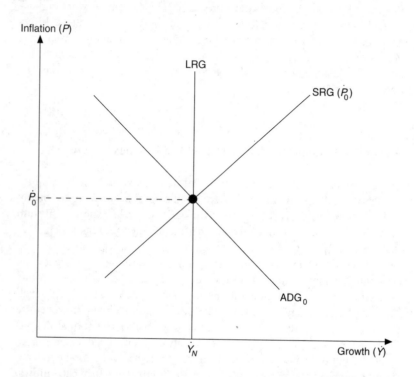

The short-run growth (SRG) schedule is drawn for a given rate of expected inflation. With the going rate of wage increases based on the expected inflation rate (for example, $\dot{P}_0$), then any (unanticipated) increase in inflation above P_0 will lead to a decline in real wages (since the rate of wage increase will fall below the rate of inflation) and an increase in growth above $\dot{Y}_N$ that is, the economy will slide up the short-run growth schedule, SRG ($\dot{P}_0$). In the long run, however, as inflationary expectations adjust, the short-run growth schedule will shift upwards as the new, higher rate of inflation becomes reflected in the going rate of wage increase.

The aggregate demand growth (ADG) schedule in the dynamic model is drawn for a given rate of growth of aggregate demand, rather than for an absolute level of aggregate demand. It is downward-sloping for the reason that, all other things being equal, for a given rate of growth of aggregate demand the higher the rate of inflation, the slower the rate of growth of demand for real goods and services (that is, output), and vice versa. That is, since:

$$AD = PY$$

then,

$$\dot{AD} = \dot{P} + \dot{Y}$$

In Figure 5.8, the aggregate demand growth schedule, ADG_0, is simply the schedule for the rate of growth of aggregate demand where:

$$\dot{AD_0} = \dot{P_0} + \dot{Y_N}$$

An increase in the rate of growth of aggregate demand shifts the aggregate demand growth schedule to the right, and vice versa.

Consider now a stylised business cycle and its impact on economic growth (see Figure 5.9). Suppose that the economy is in long-run equilibrium at point 0, with inflation (and inflationary expectations) equal to $\dot{P_0}$ and growth at its natural rate, Y_N,. Aggregate demand is growing steadily (at a rate equal to $\dot{P_0} = \dot{Y_N}$,), with the aggregate demand growth schedule at ADG_0. Imagine now that the rate of growth of aggregate demand increases, due to, say, a more expansionary monetary policy (that is, an increase in the rate of monetary growth). The aggregate demand growth schedule shifts out to ADG_1, inflation increases to $\dot{P_1}$, and the economy slides up its short-run growth schedule, $SRG(\dot{P_0})$, to a higher rate of growth, $\dot{Y_1}$, (at point 1). This fits with the normal pattern of a economic upswing: a modest increase in inflation and an acceleration in growth above its long-run trend rate.

During an economic upswing, the growth of aggregate demand tends to feed upon itself as long as the rate of growth of output is also increasing: households experience an increase in the rate at which their incomes are growing and may be encouraged to borrow and spend more in anticipation of even higher incomes in the future (that is, the savings ratio falls). Firms enjoy an increase in their rates of sales growth, inducing them to increase their borrowing in order to invest in the extra capacity necessary to meet this rising demand. Both induced effects may (temporarily) further increase the rate of growth of aggregate demand.

During the boom phase of the business cycle, inflationary expectations (and so the rate of wage increases) begin to adjust to the earlier increase in inflation. As they do so, the short-run growth schedule shifts to the left, driving the economy towards point 2. Notice that, in the process of trying

FIGURE 5.9
The Business Cycle and its Impact on Growth

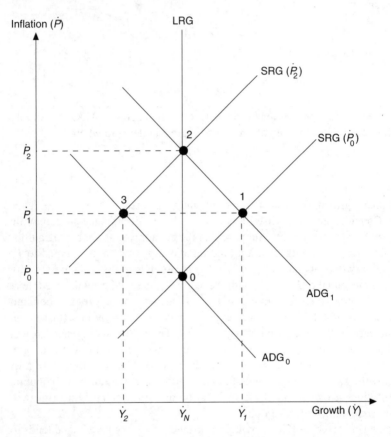

to catch up with the earlier increase in inflation, the higher rate of wage increases won by employees is passed through into a further acceleration in the inflation rate. This wage–price spiralling effect arises because the larger wage increases shift the short-run growth schedule to the left and reduce the rate of growth of output (at every rate of inflation); with an unchanged rate of growth of aggregate demand, inflation accordingly rises further. Not until inflation and inflationary expectations have finally stabilised at $\dot{P}_2$, with the short-run growth schedule at SRG($\dot{P}_2$), is the economy back in long-run equilibrium. During the wage–price spiral that typically characterises a boom (as in Britain in 1989–90), growth gradually returns to its natural rate, $\dot{Y}_N$.

In principle, the economy could achieve a 'soft landing', with growth settling at its long-run trend rate and the higher rate of aggregate demand growth translating wholly into higher inflation (in this case, P_2) at point 2. However, if the government is unwilling to tolerate a permanently higher rate of inflation, it may return to a more restrictive monetary policy. Moreover, the induced increase in consumption and investment spending which, during the upswing, typically reinforces the effect of expansionary monetary policy on the rate of growth of aggregate demand, is likely to be reversed once growth begins to slow. The so-called 'feel-good' factors of an increase in the growth of household income and an acceleration in the growth of corporate sales disappear. Households experience a slowdown in the rate of growth of income; firms find themselves with over-capacity as sales growth falls; both sectors cut back their expenditure plans accordingly. For all these reasons, as the economy returns to its trend rate of growth and inflation peaks, the rate of growth of aggregate demand will tend to fall back (for example, to ADG_0).

With the slowdown in the growth of aggregate demand and wage increases now being negotiated on the basis of the higher inflation rate, $\dot{P}_2$, the economy slides back down the short-run growth schedule, SRG ($\dot{P}_2$) into recession (point 3). Growth slumps below its trend rate to Y_2 and inflation eases back to $\dot{P}_1$). In the absence of a recovery in the rate of growth of aggregate demand (for example, led by another period of expansionary monetary policy), the economy experiences a continuing recession, with growth below trend, only returning to Y_N as inflationary expectations (and the rate of increase of wages) adjust downwards and the short-run growth schedule begins to shift back to SRG($\dot{P}_0$)), restoring the economy to equilibrium at point 0. This final phase of the business cycle may last several years, given the resistance of trades unions to attempts to reduce the real wages of their members. Table 5.8 summarises the main features of a typical business cycle.

TABLE 5.8
Economic Growth in a Stylised Business Cycle

	Economic Growth	*Inflation*
Upswing (from points 0–1)	Increasing above *YN*	Rising
Boom (from points 1–2)	Decreasing to *YN*	Rising
Recession (from points 2–3)	Decreasing below *YN*	Falling
Recovery (from points 3–0)	Increasing to *YN*	Falling

Appendix 2: The Aggregate Production Function

The aggregate production function is shown as:

$$Y = AK^\alpha L^\beta \qquad (5.1)$$

where: Y = output
A = level of technology
K = capital stock
α = capital elasticity of output
L = labour stock
β = labour elasticity of output

You will no doubt be familiar with other elasticity concepts such as the price elasticity of demand, which can be written as:

$$\frac{\Delta q}{\Delta p} \times \frac{p}{q} \text{ or } \frac{dq}{dp} \times \frac{p}{q}$$

if we use differentials.

We can prove from equation (5.1) that β, for example, is the labour elasticity of output.

Differentiating equation (5.1) with respect to labour:

$$\frac{dY}{dL} = AK^\alpha \beta L^{\beta-1} \qquad (5.2)$$

Rearranging the right-hand side of this equation gives:

$$AK^\alpha \beta L^{\beta-1} = AK^\alpha \beta \frac{L^\beta}{L} \qquad (5.3)$$

Since, from equation (5.1) $Y = Ak^\alpha L^\beta$, equation (5.3) can be re-written as:

$$AK^\alpha \beta \frac{L^\beta}{L} = Y \frac{\beta}{L}$$

or

$$AK^\alpha \beta L^{\beta-1} = Y \frac{\beta}{L}$$

Returning to equation (5.2):

$$\frac{dY}{dL} = AK^\alpha \beta L^{\beta-1} = Y \frac{\beta}{L}$$

which can be rearranged to give:

$$\frac{dY}{dL} \times \frac{L}{Y} = \beta \tag{5.4}$$

The term on the left of equation (5.4) is similar to our familiar price elasticity of demand formula, but this time it is a relationship between output and labour and not price and quantity.

The term $\frac{dY}{dL} \times \frac{L}{Y}$ is the labour elasticity of output, therefore $\beta =$ labour elasticity of output. Similarly, we could undertake the same process to deduce that α is the capital elasticity of output.

Keynesian Prescriptions for Economic Growth 6

Between 1945 and the mid-1970s, the ideas of John Maynard Keynes represented the prevailing orthodoxy in economic theory. Keynes argued that, at a macroeconomic level, the operation of the 'invisible hand' alone was unlikely to result in the economy reaching and settling at 'full employment'. Price and wage stickiness, informational asymmetries and the absence of futures markets would all tend to prevent free markets from working smoothly. The implications of this theory for economic growth was that the free market would fail to generate the economic conditions, and the subsequent rates of investment in R&D and capital, necessary to achieve a socially desirable rate of economic growth. This chapter examines the basic mechanics of the Keynesian model and shows how it implies that direct state intervention, both to avoid prolonged slumps and correct market failure on the supply side, is necessary if the economy is to fulfil its growth potential.

The 45° Line Model

The principles of 'Keynesianism' are most familiarly expressed in the well-known '45° line diagram'. Figure 6.1 illustrates the traditional 45° line model. The 45° line shows points at which the equilibrium condition, namely that planned expenditure (E) – i.e., the sum of planned consumption (C), investment (I), government spending (G) and net exports $(X - M)$ – equals planned output (Y). The expenditure function $(C + I + G + X - M)$ shows how aggregate planned expenditure varies with actual output.

FIGURE 6.1
Keynesian Expenditure/Income/Output model

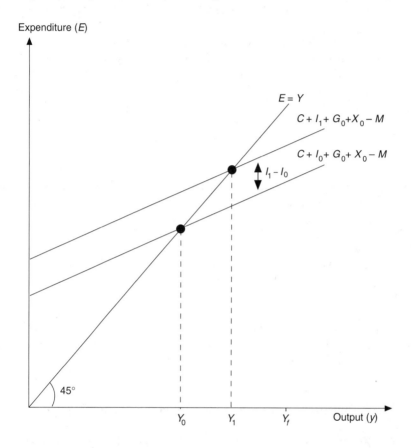

Although investment, government spending and exports are assumed to be exogenous (i.e., invariant with respect to output), consumption varies (positively) and imports (negatively) with output, the extent of which depends on their relative marginal propensities. Overall, a rise in output induces a net increase in planned expenditure, so that the expenditure schedule is upward-sloping.

Figure 6.1 shows that, given the exogenous levels of investment (I_0), government spending (G_0) and exports (X_0), and the relevant propensities to consume ($\delta C/\delta Y$) and import ($\delta M/\delta Y$), the equilibrium level of income is Y_0. An increase in any of the exogenous components of expenditure leads to an increase in output. For example, an increase in investment from I_0 to I_1 shifts the expenditure schedule vertically upwards (by I_1–I_0), increasing the equilibrium level of output from Y_0 to Y_1. Note that the increase in expenditure translates directly into an increase in output; none of the extra spending is dissipated in higher wages and prices. The only circumstances in the 45° line model in which an increase in expenditure fails to materialise as an increase in output is if the economy is at 'full employment' (Y_f), when by definition all resources are being fully utilised. In this case, an increase in, say, investment which raises the point at which the 45° line and the expenditure schedule intersect above Y_f would lead to inflation.

In terms of the aggregate supply and demand model discussed above, the assumption of price (and wage) rigidity in the 45° line model is equivalent to an aggregate supply (AS) schedule which is completely horizontal up to Y_f, beyond which it is vertical (i.e., any additional increase in aggregate demand beyond this point leads only to an increase in prices – and wages – with output unresponsive). Figures 6.2a and 6.2b illustrate the relationship between the 45° line diagram and the underlying aggregate supply and demand diagram. The aggregate demand (AD) schedule in Figure 6.2b is downward-sloping because, as the price level increases (with a given money supply), interest rates rise, investment falls and the planned expenditure schedule shifts downwards from $(C + I + G + X - M)$ (P_0) to $(C + I + G + X - M)(P_1)$. (NB: the relationship between investment and interest rates is discussed more fully in Chapters 7 and 8.)

The Implications of the 45° Line Model for Economic Growth

The Keynesian view of the economy dominated the way that British policy was made in the period 1945–79. Keynesian economists argued that, of the private-sector components of aggregate demand, investment in particular would tend to be highly unstable. Fluctuations in investment would thus give rise to wild swings in output in the absence of government intervention. In particular, Keynesians were concerned that, left to its own devices, aggregate demand might fall, causing the economy to lodge below its natural rate of output for extended periods. With wages 'sticky' downwards, rather than falling to clear the labour market and – by allowing firms to pass on the reduction in labour costs in the form of lower prices, thereby pushing the economy back towards its natural rate output – the economy would instead suffer persistent unemployment and sluggish (or zero) growth. Keynesians also recognised that spontaneous increases in

FIGURE 6.2
Aggregate Demand, Aggregate Supply in Keynesian Model

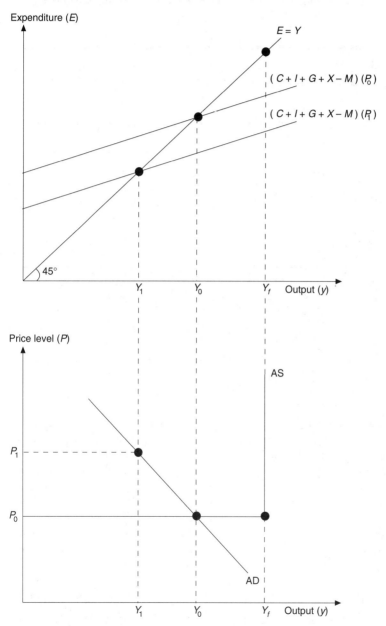

aggregate demand might equally well lead to inflation, as output increased above its natural rate, but they tended to regard the possibility of unemployment as the greater danger. Table 6.1 illustrates the volatility of the various components of domestic spending for the major economies.

TABLE 6.1
Variability of Domestic Demand and Output, 1975–1991 (at constant prices)

	Consumption	Investment	Government Spending	Output
Britain	2.0	6.0	2.8	2.7
France	1.2	3.8	1.5	1.2
Germany	0.6	3.4	0.7	1.3
Italy	1.0	2.7	0.7	0.9
Japan	1.2	1.7	1.6	0.8
United States	1.1	4.1	2.9	1.6

NOTE   Variability as measured by coefficient of variation.
SOURCE   Burda, M. and Wyplosz, C. (1993) *Macroeconomics: A European Text* (London: Oxford University Press).

Keynesians accordingly recommended that governments should aim to stabilise the level of aggregate demand at the natural rate of output, neutralising fluctuations in the private-sector components of spending by appropriate adjustments in government spending, tax rates and interest rates. Discretionary fiscal and monetary policy of this type is normally referred to as 'finetuning'. Not only was this approach to demand management policy urged as the only way of avoiding prolonged periods of economic stagnation (high unemployment and slow growth), but Keynesians also argued that stabilising aggregate demand was the best way to promote a high and stable level of investment. Because investment in research and development (R&D) and physical and human capital is so sensitive to expectations about the future level of demand for firms' finished products (see also Chapter 8 below), Keynesians claimed that only by ensuring a high, stable level of aggregate demand would firms have the confidence they needed to invest for the future. Table 6.2 shows that the variability of the British economy, in terms of the key variables of growth, inflation and interest rates, has exceeded that of its major two European competitors.

TABLE 6.2
Variability of the British Economy, 1975–91

	Growth	Inflation	Interest Rates
Britain	2.6	0.8	0.4
France	1.7	0.5	0.3
Germany	1.9	0.8	0.4

NOTE Variability as measured by coefficient of variation.
SOURCE As Table 6.1.

Consistent with this view of the world, which was based on the proposition that the unbridled operation of free markets would fail to propel the economy towards its natural rate of output efficiently following changes in aggregate demand, Keynesians argued that direct state intervention in the supply side was also essential if countries were to maximise their growth potential. In other words, they believed that market failure was so widespread that it could only be tackled via extensive government involvement in the workings of the private sector.

Market Failure and Externalities

The intellectual case for market intervention is rooted in basic microeconomics and the concept of market failure. The market will fail to allocate resources efficiently whenever the private costs and benefits faced by producers and consumers do not completely reflect the social costs and benefits to society as a whole. For example, coal-fired power stations impose a cost on society – in the form of the environmental damage caused by acid rain – over and above the private opportunity costs (i.e., the cost of land, labour, capital, etc.) which falls upon the producer. The additional social cost is known as an externality or spillover effect and, being a cost, is negative. Conversely, society enjoys a wider benefit from the successful treatment of a patient with a contagious disease – in so far as the risk of other individuals being infected is reduced – over and above the private benefits which accrue to the patient concerned. The extra social benefit is a positive externality or spillover effect.

In both these examples, the presence of externalities will lead to market failure, because the free market will tend to allocate resources in a way that is socially suboptimal. Coal-fired power stations will be operated where marginal private cost equals marginal revenue (see Figure 6.3), producing a profit-maximising amount Q_0. In fact, the social optimum is where marginal social cost intersects marginal revenue, which would give rise to a lower quantity, Q_1, being produced. In other words, negative externalities result in socially excessive levels of production and consumption. On the other hand, the consumption of health care by those afflicted with contagious diseases will tend to be less than is socially desirable. Figure 6.4 shows that utility-maximising individuals would demand an amount Q_0, which is where marginal private revenue (i.e., marginal private benefits) equals marginal cost. In fact, the socially efficient level of consumption would be Q_1, where the marginal social revenue (or benefit) schedule intersects marginal cost. Positive externalities thus lead to under-production and consumption.

FIGURE 6.3
The Case of Negative Externalities

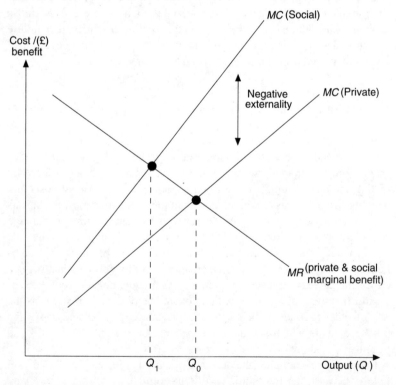

FIGURE 6.4
The Case of Positive Externalities

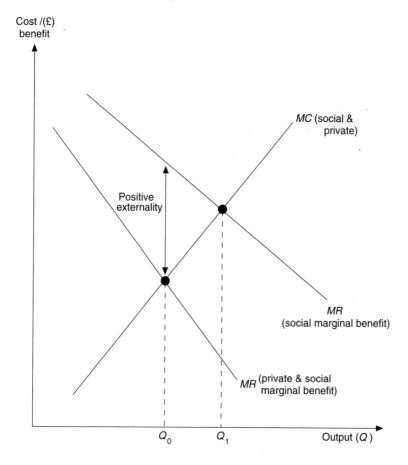

Keynesians argue that many of the key determinants of economic growth are plagued by positive externalities, so that the free market will tend to underinvest in R&D and physical and human capital. As a result, the growth rate will be slower than socially optimal. Consider basic R&D. Expenditure on pioneering R&D to develop new products and processes is expensive and innovating firms are only imperfectly protected from imitators by patent laws (which prohibit rivals 'cloning' the innovators' new products). Patent law is often difficult to enforce and followers have a significant cost advantage over the innovator, since they do not have to recoup the initial R&D costs. When Sony first launched the 'Walkman' cassette-player, for example, it temporarily enjoyed a monopoly position and prices in real terms were 400–500 per cent higher than they are today. Within months of the product reaching the market, however, it was followed by a host of cheaper cassette-players from rival manufacturers, which quickly drove down the market price. Sony's R&D thus had a positive spillover effect from the point of view of other firms. Since Sony could not prevent the technology it had invented from becoming public knowledge, the other firms profited from Sony's R&D without having to pay for it; in other words, the benefit to society as a whole far exceeded the private benefits to Sony.

Given the presence of positive externalities, Keynesians argued, the amount of R&D undertaken by firms in aggregate is likely to be socially suboptimal, with many firms preferring to wait for their rivals to make the technological breakthroughs. It is significant that, in Japan, where the corporate system of *keiretzu* ties together otherwise independent companies through a complex series of interlocking directorships and shareholdings, companies do not have the same incentive to free-ride on the R&D of others and Japan is a clearly established world leader in high-tech industries. In Britain, on the other hand, Keynesians concluded that the same effect could only be achieved through government intervention.

Training and education may also be subject to similar effects (see also Chapter 9). Imagine that in the absence of publicly provided training and education, a private company decides to offer training services to subscribing firms. While each firm would pay to send its staff on the training courses, each guesses (rightly) that, by not paying, the benefits can be enjoyed by 'free-riding' at their neighbours' expense, since they may be able to poach trained workers from their rivals by paying only slightly above the present market wage. As a result, many firms refuse to subscribe and the ensuing service is socially suboptimal. An alternative solution would be to publicly provide the training, financing it with a tax which each company will willingly pay, in the knowledge that the scheme constrains their neighbours to join with them in a collectively advantageous enterprise.

Information and Economic Co-ordination

The Keynesians also believed that the 'invisible hand' was ill-suited to the task of co-ordinating investment across a modern economy. For the car industry, for example, to invest in new, high-tech plant and equipment, its managers had to be confident of the future demand for their products – a guarantee provided by the government's commitment to maintain a high level of aggregate demand. But if the industry's expansion were not to be choked off by shortages of machinery and skilled workers, it required that the capital goods industry, in turn, be geared up to provide the extra machine tools needed by car producers; and that the school system equip school leavers with the knowledge to use the new machinery. How was this degree of co-ordination to be achieved across a complex, inter-dependent economy, Keynesians asked?

Given the long lead times between the decision to produce and the delivery of the finished product, Keynesians doubted that price signals alone would work to co-ordinate the plans of different sectors. How were machine tool makers to know that the car industry intended a major expansion? When the increase in investment started to take place, the car industry would accordingly find the machine tool sector without the capacity to respond. While shortages would drive up the price of machine tools, thereby stimulating an increase in output, it might take months, even years, before supply fully responded to the increased demand from the car industry. Similarly, it may take years for local schools to adjust the mix of their vocational training courses to meet the changing needs of employers like the car industry.

In the meantime, the intended expansion of the car industry, while having set in motion increases in the capacity of its suppliers, would have been initially held back by the shortage of machine tools and skilled labour. Disadvantaged in this way, the car industry might find itself losing ground to overseas competitors, forcing it to reassess its plans for expansion. By the time the extra machine tools and skilled labour became available, the domestic car industry might be so weakened that it could no longer carry out its original plans. In other words, when there are long time lags between firms receiving price signals and actually responding with changes in production, events may have moved on so that by the time the supply-side responses actually come, they are no longer appropriate.

Keynesians concluded that the invisible hand was therefore likely to be incapable of co-ordinating the investment decisions across the economy in a way that would maximise the rate of economic growth. While the guarantee of high and stable levels of aggregate demand would undoubtedly help, Keynesians argued that governments should play a more explicit role in ensuring balanced growth. This attitude to the functioning of the economy became influential in the early 1960s, following the apparent success of national economic planning in countries as diverse as the former Soviet Union, Japan and France.

The Keynesian Prescription for Economic Growth

Keynesians were highly sceptical of the ability of free markets to function efficiently. They argued that the widespread existence of externalities and market failure and the inability of the price mechanism to carry the information necessary to co-ordinate economic decision-making would result in suboptimal rates of economic growth. Persuaded by the Keynesians' diagnosis of Britain's economic ills, successive governments during the period 1945–79 concentrated their growth-promoting efforts on three main fronts:

1. attempts to plan the economy;
2. taking firms into public ownership;
3. government-directed investment and industrial restructuring.

Indicative Planning

In the early post-war years, national economic planning was used to (apparently) good effect by both communist and Western governments. The experience of the Soviet Union was particularly impressive in this regard. Although it eventually ran into terminal difficulties, for the first 50 years after the 1917 revolution the Soviet Union recorded an impressive rate of economic growth, transforming its once peasant economy into a global superpower. The dominant feature of the Soviet economy was the degree of central control, with government planners working out detailed, mutually consistent plans for the output of each enterprise over a five-year period. If the planners decided that the state required an increase in car production, they would ensure that appropriate adjustments were automatically made to the output targets for all supplying sectors, including machine tools and vocational training. By replacing the invisible hand of the price mechanism by direct orders from the centre, many British economists in the 1960s felt that the Soviet Union had overcome the co-ordination problems that they believed plagued a market economy.

At the same time, free market economies such as Japan and France also appeared to have used a more dilute form of central planning, thereby allowing them to achieve higher growth rates than Britain in the period 1945–60. The so-called 'indicative plans' of these latter countries worked by 'indicating' to private companies the output targets at which they should aim. The logic was that, if each firm produced in line with its nationally set goals, the economy as a whole would be able to grow in a co-ordinated, balanced fashion. These indicative plans were normally agreed by collaboration between the government's planners, employers' federations and representatives of organised labour. Although they were nominally voluntary, both Japan and France used a variety of 'sticks' (e.g., withdrawal of state contracts from companies that failed to participate) and 'carrots' (e.g., tax incentives and cheap credit) to encourage compliance with the plan.

Inspired by the apparent success of central planning, Keynesian economists urged successive British governments to develop nation-wide indicative plans to accelerate economic growth. The high point of planning in Britain came in the mid-1960s, when the 1959–64 Conservative Government set up a tripartite planning body – comprising government ministers, the Confederation of British Industry and the Trades Union Congress – to agree a national plan. The body existed until 1992 (when it was finally abolished) in the shape of the National Economic Development Committee (NEDC). The subsequent 1964–70 Labour Government inherited the initiative with great enthusiasm, establishing a new department of state (the Department of Economic Affairs) charged with drawing up a definitive plan, which was published amid great publicity in 1965.

In the event, the plan failed miserably. Lacking the infrastructure of fiscal 'carrots' and 'sticks' enjoyed by their French and Japanese counterparts, there was little the government could do to promote compliance with the plan, other than exhort the private sector to invest and expand in the public good. When the government was forced to sharply deflate the economy by a sterling crisis in 1966, thereby temporarily depressing profits and employment, the plan's credibility collapsed and it was quietly abandoned. The notion that the price mechanism was incapable of co-ordinating investment decisions lived on throughout the 1970s, however, and although later governments never again attempted a national plan, indicative planning at the sectoral level continued until 1979.

Nationalisation

The major driving force behind the wave of nationalisation that took place immediately after the war was primarily ideological, rather than economic. Socialists believed that, by taking control of the 'commanding heights' of the economy – electricity, gas, coal, steel, rail, shipbuilding, etc. – the government could direct the economy as a whole, without having to nationalise all the thousands of smaller private sector companies as well. Instead of pursuing private profit, productive enterprises were to be channelled into meeting public needs.

Nationalisation did, however, fit with the theoretical views of many Keynesians, who believed that the free market was unable to maximise the nation's growth potential. They pointed to the run-down state of many companies (e.g., the private railway companies) prior to nationalisation, arguing that short-termism or lack of confidence on the part of private owners had prevented necessary investment in plant and equipment taking place. Once in the public sector, with the backing of government, these staple industries would be able to enjoy higher levels of investment and productivity growth.

Keynesians also regarded public ownership as economically superior to private ownership in the case of monopolistic industries. Figure 6.5 shows that a profit-maximising monopolist will set marginal cost (*MC*) equal to marginal revenue (*MR*) at point *A*, thereby making super-normal profit (shown by area P_mCBD in Figure 6.5). In contrast, if the industry com-

FIGURE 6.5
The Advantages of Publicly Owned Monopolies

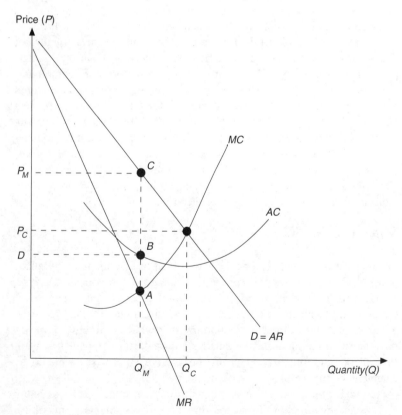

prised a number of competitive firms (in which case, the marginal cost curve shown in Figure 6.5 would be the sum of all the individual firms' marginal cost curves – i.e., the industry supply curve), each firm would produce where its marginal cost was equal to price (average revenue) and output would be higher (Q_c rather than Q_m) and prices lower (P_c rather than P_m). This analysis highlights the way in which private monopolists profit-maximise by restricting output and charging higher prices. Such an outcome is economically inefficient, since it means that, in equilibrium, the marginal cost of the last unit is *less* than consumers would have been prepared to pay (i.e., its price). Social welfare could therefore be increased by expanding output up to the point where the marginal cost of production is just equal to the value consumers place on the marginal unit of output (which is at Q_c).

Keynesians argued that breaking up private monopolies was likely to raise costs, since a number of small, competing firms would be unable to benefit from the economies of scale enjoyed by a single, large producer. Addressing the problem of private monopoly in this way would therefore raise the industry's costs (shifting up the marginal cost for a competitive industry above that of the monopolist in Figure 6.5) and dissipating the gains from greater allocative efficiency. It was better, they concluded, to simply bring the private monopoly into public ownership, where its management could be instructed to pursue socially optimal, as opposed to profit-maximising, goals. In the case of Figure 6.5, the government could direct the state monopoly to set its marginal cost equal to price and produce a level of output, Q_c. The alternative is a cumbersome regulatory system, which forces a private monopolist to behave in the public interest, with all the attendant problems that entails.

Such considerations are especially important in the case of so-called 'natural' monopolies (i.e., industries with declining long-run marginal cost curves, in which one single producer is the inevitable outcome of the free market). Figure 6.6 illustrates a situation in which marginal and average costs decline continuously over all feasible levels of output. The problem is that the economically efficient level of output, Q_c, would result in the producer making a loss (equal to area P_cEFG), rather than the profit of P_mCBD enjoyed by the same enterprise under private ownership. While it is technically possible that a regulatory authority could force a private monopolist to operate at a loss-making level of output and then pay compensating subsidies, it is clearly much more practical to operate such a company within the public sector, where it could produce an economically efficient level of output with consequent losses covered by the taxpayer.

Inspired by such ideological and theoretical considerations, the size of the public sector steadily grew until 1979. Although Labour governments

FIGURE 6.6
Price/Output Equilibrium under a Natural Monopoly

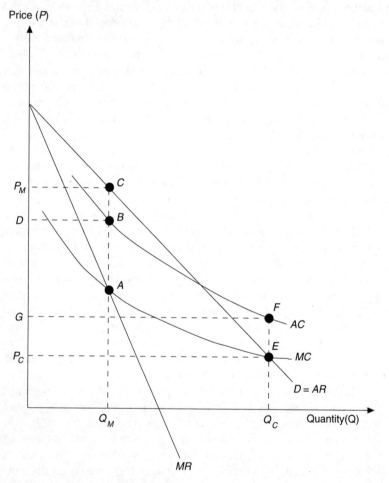

nationalised more enthusiastically than their Conservative counterparts, the latter also took into public ownership major employers like Rolls-Royce, preferring to use public money to nationalise and restructure them rather than allow them to go out of business. By 1979, public enterprises accounted for more than 30 per cent of total employment.

Government Direction of Investment

Although 'Keynesian' governments never succeeded in creating a sufficiently comprehensive infrastructure of carrots and sticks to make indicative planning workable, they nevertheless developed quite a battery of instruments designed to prod private-sector companies into investing more in physical and human capital. For example, although successive governments argued over the relative merits of using tax allowances as opposed to direct subsidies to promote capital spending, until 1979 the proposition that the private sector needed an additional incentive to invest (over and above the expected rate of return on the project itself) was never seriously challenged.

Similarly, there were various schemes to promote corporate spending on training. It was generally felt that, unless the government created positive incentives for firms to train their workers, firms would tend to 'poach' ready-trained labour from their rivals rather than train themselves, with the result that total expenditure on investment in human capital would be lower than socially desirable. Successive governments used a mixture of direct subsidies (e.g., so much per worker trained) and levies (i.e., a 'tax' designed to raise revenue from individual firms for training at the industry level).

In addition, the government also on occasion took the lead in funding R&D projects in private-sector firms. For example, in the 1960s, the British and French governments collaborated to finance the development of *Concorde*, the world's first supersonic commercial airliner. In the 1970s, the Labour Government established the National Enterprise Board, which lent money (by taking an equity stake) to emerging, high-technology companies, in an effort to stimulate R&D in 'leading-edge' sectors like computers.

An Assessment of Keynesian Growth Policies

From 1945 until 1979, macroeconomic policy in Britain followed the policy prescriptions of the Keynesian tradition. Demand management was used to try and stabilise aggregate demand at a level consistent with the natural rate of output, although in practice political pressures often resulted in governments overstimulating demand, temporarily forcing unemployment below its natural rate at the cost of higher inflation in the longer term. While an important justification of finetuning was that it promoted economic growth by providing the conditions in which firms could invest with confidence, Keynesians also prescribed a raft of explicit growth policies. These were justified on the grounds of widespread market failure and included indicative planning, nationalisation and various measures, both indirect (e.g., fiscal carrots and sticks) and direct, to stimulate R&D and investment in physical and human capital.

These policies were not without their critics. New Classical economists attacked finetuning as inflationary and counterproductive, rejecting the notion that the private sector was inherently unstable and claiming that wages adjusted rapidly to changes in prices. More significantly, they also dismissed the proposition that the price mechanism was unable to co-ordinate economic activity and generate the optimal levels of investment, claiming instead that Britain's poor growth record reflected excessive government interference in the economy, rather than any inherent deficiency in the private sector. They alleged that the growth of the public sector, which took output and employment decisions on non-commercial grounds, and the increase in taxes necessary to finance the welfare state had seriously damaged the incentives to invest. It is to this critique of the Keynesian era and the policy recommendations of the New Classical school that Chapter 7 now turns.

New Classical Prescriptions for Economic Growth

In the 1970s, the Keynesian theoretical orthodoxy came under increasing attack from the 'New Classical' school. The dissenters, led by the Chicago economist Milton Friedman, were initially dubbed 'monetarists', due to their insistence that the basic cause of inflation was excessively rapid growth of the money supply. But as the intellectual debate unfolded, it became clear that the fundamental disagreement between the monetarists (or 'New Classical' economists) and the Keynesians lay not in the determination of aggregate demand, but rather in the shape of the aggregate supply curve and the efficiency of the private sector. This chapter discusses the New Classical economists' critique of Keynesianism and examines their policy prescriptions for economic growth, many of which have been adopted by the Conservative Government since 1979.

Keynesian versus the New Classical Economics

As noted in Chapter 6, the Keynesian orthodoxy as embodied in the famous 45° line diagram was underpinned by the assumption that the aggregate supply curve is horizontal up to the point at which full employment was reached. A horizontal aggregate supply schedule implied that, below full employment, the economy was in a state of permanent disequilibrium (notably an excess supply of labour), so that following an increase in aggregate demand, output could rise passively without putting upward pressure on prices and wages. As the New Classical economists pointed out, such an assumption was equivalent to asserting that, in a modern economy, the market mechanism fails to operate; or at least, fails to operate rapidly enough to make a *laissez-faire* approach to economic policy politically acceptable.

The New Classical economists categorically rejected this diagnosis. They argued that the private sector was inherently efficient, so that, in the absence of destabilising government intervention, labour and goods markets would clear quickly and the economy would automatically tend to its natural rate of output. They concluded, moreover, that far from being necessary to stabilise aggregate demand, discretionary demand management policy had, in fact, been positively destabilising. This was because, when aggregate demand spontaneously changed, the private sector rapidly began to adapt its price and wage-fixing behaviour. Policy adjustments by the government, which inevitably took time to implement, simply had the effect of pushing the economy further in the direction in which it was already moving, causing it to overshoot the natural rate of output and leading to either inflation or unemployment.

Moreover, to the extent that markets did not appear to clear as smoothly as New Classical economists claimed, they argued that any sluggishness was due to the interference of government, which had injected damaging distortions into the economic system. The building blocks of Keynesian-inspired state intervention – nationalisation, direct controls and regulations and high taxes – were singled out for particular criticism in this regard. In contrast to the Keynesians, who had highlighted the importance of market failure as the primary source of slow growth in the British economy, the New Classical economists stressed the need to liberate and properly reward individual enterprise.

The Rationale of New Classical Growth Policies

Like Keynesians, the New Classical school faced the task of explaining why it is that some countries undertake more research and development (R&D) and invest more in physical and human capital than others, thereby reaping the benefits of faster economic growth. In providing their answer to this conundrum, the New Classical school emphasised the importance of individual economic agents attempting to maximise their welfare subject to the constraints they faced. To the extent that government interference in the functioning of the economy – for example, by the levying of taxes, the imposition of legal restrictions and controls, etc. – necessarily altered the pattern of welfare-maximising behaviour by individual agents (including their investment in R&D and physical and human capital), the New Classical economists laid the blame for Britain's poor growth performance directly at the door of overweaning government. In this regard, the New Classical economists drew upon a long tradition of free market economic thinking, which dated back to Adam Smith's famous book, *The Wealth of Nations*.

In terms of specifically promoting economic growth, the New Classical school emphasised the need to revitalise competitive market forces and to reform laws, regulations and tax systems in order to improve the incentives for individuals to seek out productive activities. Inspired by the New Classical school, the Conservative Government that came to power in 1979 rejected the Keynesian growth policies that it inherited and introduced a raft of new measures which included:

1. the privatisation of nationalised industries;
2. the deregulation of the goods and capital markets;
3. the reform of the tax and social security system to increase incentives to work and invest;
4. legislative changes designed to liberalise the labour market; and
5. reductions in government spending and the budget deficit to prevent the 'crowding out' of private-sector investment.

Privatisation

Privatisation entails the transfer of nationalised industries to the private sector, where they can once again function in a commercial, profit-seeking environment. Table 7.1 lists the major privatisations since 1979. In total, the Conservative Government sold over £40bn of state assets over the period 1979–93. In 1979, the state held a major stake in many of Britain's most important industries, including steel, motor vehicles, aerospace, coal, railways, road haulage, air travel (e.g., British Airways), oil, telecommunications, electricity, gas and water. By 1993, however, only the coal industry (British Coal) and the railways (British Rail) remained in the state sector and both were scheduled for privatisation in the medium term. The wave of privatisation has now reduced the direct role of the state in production to one of the lowest in Europe, although it remains considerably higher than in the United States (see Table 7.2).

While ideological and political factors have influenced the privatisation programme since 1979, it nevertheless remains the case that privatisation is primarily aimed at strengthening the performance of the supply side of the economy. Ministers argue that, under public control, nationalised industries had no incentive to cut costs and respond to changing patterns of consumer demand. Since many nationalised industries enjoyed con-

TABLE 7.1
Major British Privatisations

Enterprise Privatised	Year(s)
British Petroleum	1979
British Aerospace	1980–6
Cable and Wireless	1981–5
Amersham International	1982
National Freight Corporation	1982
Britoil	1982–5
British Rail Hotels	1983
Associated British Ports	1983–4
Austin-Rover	1984–8
British Telecom	1984–91
Enterprise Oil	1984
Sealink	1984
British Shipbuilders	1985
National Bus Company	1986
British Gas	1986
Rolls Royce	1987
British Airports Authority	1987
British Airways	1987
Royal Ordnance Factories	1987
British Steel	1988–9
Water Boards	1989–90
Electricity Distributors	1990
Electricity Generators	1991

SOURCE   HM Treasury (1991), *Public Expenditure White Paper*, HMSO.

siderable monopoly power, they could easily achieve the crude financial objectives imposed on them by successive governments (e.g., achieving a specified rate of return on capital investment) by manipulating their prices, rather than by cutting overmanning and producing more efficiently.

Nationalised industries in the 1970s were characterised by considerable 'X-inefficiency' (i.e., bureaucratic waste), overmanning and ill-directed investment. Productivity growth in the nationalised sector lagged well behind that in the private sector and many enterprises made heavy financial losses which absorbed huge amounts of taxpayers' money. To

TABLE 7.2
The Role of the State in Direct Production

Country	Per cent of GDP Produced by Nationalised Industries (%)
Britain	11
France	17
Germany	11
Italy	14
United States	1

SOURCE   *The Economist*, 'Business in Europe', 8 June 1991.

the general public, both at home and abroad, British nationalised industries were synonymous with over-priced, poor-quality service.

However, given that most privatised industries continue to enjoy a significant degree of monopoly power, it is not immediately clear how precisely privatisation was intended to spur incumbent managements to greater efficiency. After all, the morning after privatisation, companies like British Telecom and British Gas – with the same managers and staff and effectively unchallenged control of national, integrated distribution networks – faced no greater competition for customers than they had while in the public sector.

For such companies, the New Classical economists argued, the impetus to greater competition and efficiency lay in the new vulnerability of privatised enterprises to hostile takeover bids on the stock market. This is because the shareholders, who continue to hold their shares in the company only as long as the management run their affairs in a way that maximises their return, will revolt against a board of directors that does not act in their interests. In principle, the shareholders could spontaneously evict a non-profit-maximising management at an annual general meeting. In practice, they are more likely to sell their shares, depressing the company's share price and encouraging outsiders – who believe they can make better use of the company's assets – to buy up the unwanted shares and impose their own managers in place of the incumbents. For monopolistic companies, it is the threat of such a hostile takeover, rather than the need to defend market share against rival producers, that proponents of privatisation argue is the main inducement to greater efficiency.

The Deregulation of Goods and Financial Markets

Government regulations in the goods and financial markets are normally justified as a means of protecting consumers (and workers, in the case of health and safety legislation) from the consequences of unscrupulous firms and employers, who seek to exploit their monopoly power or abuse the power that their privileged access to information gives them. There are numerous legal cases of firms which have knowingly sold products which have killed or maimed customers (e.g., General Motors, which sold pick-up trucks in the 1980s with exposed petrol tanks which were vulnerable in side impacts), or exposed their workers to unsafe working conditions (e.g., certain US nuclear power generators, which have been found guilty of exposing their employees to unsafe levels of radiation). For this reason, free markets are widely regulated by health and safety laws and consumer protection legislation.

However, New Classical economists argue that many regulations, while ostensibly aimed at protecting consumers and workers, are in fact primarily calculated to limit competition and act in the interests of established suppliers. Such regulations, which are outlawed under the Treaty of Rome, have been the subject of considerable investigation by the European Commission, which has unearthed numerous cases in defence of the New Classical view. For example, until recently German 'purity laws' had the effect of excluding otherwise perfectly safe beers brewed abroad from the German market, allowing local breweries to earn economic rents. Similarly, the British practice of allowing only licensed, Ministry-inspected dairy farms to sell fresh milk in the British market had the effect of barring French producers. Both regulations may once have been in the public interest, but in recent years, the only beneficiaries, which lobbied very hard against the European Commission for their maintenance, were the producer groups whose excess profits the laws protected.

Deregulation thus involves reducing the number of regulations by removing those that serve to restrict competition and do little to enhance the safety of customers or workers. The objectives of deregulation are to increase competition between existing suppliers and to make markets more 'contestable', by facilitating new entrants (for example, by forcing British Telecom to allow Mercury to use its lines in order to compete for business). Such deregulation should, the New Classical economists argue, reduce costs and stimulate the provision of new services for which there is a demand. Early examples of deregulation in Britain are buses (liberalised by the 1980 Transport Act) and the Stock Exchange, which was opened up in 1986 by 'Big Bang'. More recently, the European Commission's '1992' programme to 'complete the internal market' eliminated a raft of non-tariff barriers to intra-EC trade between 1985–92, many of which were competition-stifling regulations of the type discussed above.

Tax and Social Security Reforms

Whether a tax is levied according to a person's ability to pay or according to his or her expenditure, it reduces the rate of return that individual obtains from market activities; for example, working for a wage or investing in shares or other assets with taxable yields. The New Classical argument is that, as a consequence of taxation, people will be less willing to engage in market activities, as well as shifting into market activities that are less heavily taxed. They will also risk not reporting all their income to the tax authorities; in other words, they will work in the 'black' or 'shadow' economy. Table 7.3 shows estimates of the size of the black economy for the main industrial countries. Although there is considerable disagreement about the accuracy of these estimates, there is a consensus that the size of the black economy has been growing in many countries in recent years.

TABLE 7.3
Estimates of the Size of the Black Economy (% of GDP)

Country	Average Estimate
Britain	9
France	4
Germany	14
Italy	15
United States	15

SOURCE   OECD (1990) *Economic et Statistique*, Institute National de la Státistique et des Etudes Economiques, Paris.

Concern about the inefficiency caused by excessively high marginal tax rates inspired tax reforms in the 1980s in a number of countries. The tax structure refers to the different kinds of activities that are taxed and the differential tax rates applied – for example, what kind of income is taxed and what rates of tax different income earners have to pay (see Table 7.4 for details of the tax structures in the main industrial countries). Indirect taxes also distort choices. If a good is taxed more heavily than others, consumers will buy less of it and switch to other goods. This reduces consumers' utility because they would prefer, in the absence of the tax, to buy more of the good.

TABLE 7.4
Taxes as a % of GDP, 1991

Country	Indirect Tax	Income Tax	Social Security	Other	Total Tax
Britain	11	10	6	9	36
France	12	6	19	7	44
Germany	11	11	13	2	37
Italy	11	9	13	7	40

SOURCE   OECD (1992) *National Accounts*, Paris.

New Classical economists argue that taxes on labour – both social security contributions and income taxes – are particularly damaging because of their direct impact on the supply of, and demand for, labour. Table 7.5 shows the marginal and average taxes on labour for the main industrial countries. Inspired by the New Classical school, Britain's labour taxes are now amongst the lowest in Europe. The economic effect of income taxes, together with the disincentive effects of high social security benefits to the unemployed (of which the New Classical economists are also highly critical) are analysed in detail in Chapter 9 below.

TABLE 7.5
Taxes on Labour (%), 1988

Country	Employers' Social Security Tax	Employees' Social Security Tax	Maximum Marginal Income Tax Tax Rate	Average Income Tax Rate
Britain	14.1	6.8	60.0	21.2
France	39.3	20.9	58.0	16.5
Germany	24.3	19.9	56.0	23.7
Italy	37.3	11.2	62.0	33.8
Japan	16.2	8.8	88.0	15.3
United States	19.9	7.3	38.0	20.8

SOURCE   OECD (1990) *Economic Outlook*, August, Paris.

Labour Market Reform

Labour market reform was at the forefront of the Conservative Government's growth strategy during the 1980s. Ministers variously accused trade unions of inhibiting economic progress and blunting Britain's overseas competitiveness by the use of restrictive work practices and overmanning and preventing the flexible operation of the labour market, by holding wages above their market-clearing levels and thereby causing higher unemployment.

The Conservative Government's attempts to reform the labour market have proved electorally popular. By the late 1970s, there was a growing public conviction that the trade unions had become too powerful. This view was reinforced during the so-called 'winter of discontent' of 1978–79, when there were major disputes in the health service and the road haulage industry as unions challenged the Labour Government's pay guidelines. Unions were also widely perceived as refusing to abandon restrictive practices, thereby hindering technological change and depressing the growth of labour productivity. Since 1979, a series of statutes has placed restrictions on trade union activity. The objectives and effects of these reforms is considered in more detail in Chapter 9.

Government Spending, Budget Deficits and Crowding Out

Under the approving eye of Keynesian policy advisors, post-war governments in the period 1945–79 frequently deliberately ran budget deficits as a means of stimulating aggregate demand. During recessions, when investment tended to fall, governments typically responded by either cutting taxes (with government spending unchanged) or increasing government spending (with taxes unchanged). The result was a net stimulus to aggregate demand. Conversely, during an economic upswing, spending would be cut or taxes increased.

The new classical school was deeply critical of such fiscal 'fine-tuning', arguing that Keynesians failed to take into account the damaging side-effects on private-sector investment. At its simplest, the New Classical economists believed that budget deficits, by increasing interest rates, worked to reduce investment. The concept of crowding out is closely related to the 'multiplier': the greater the degree of crowding out, the lower will be the government expenditure multiplier. The relationship between the two concepts can be summarised as follows (the symbol δ means 'changes in'):

$$\text{multiplier}\,(k) = \delta Y\,/\,\delta G$$

and, crowding out (expressed as %) = $(\delta G - \delta Y)/\delta G \times 100$; therefore,

$$\% \text{ crowding out} = (1 - \text{multiplier}) \times 100.$$

The relationship between the critical values of the two concepts is set out in Table 7.6.

TABLE 7.6
The Multiplier and Crowding Out

Value of the Multiplier equals	Crowding out
$k > 1$	negative crowding out (i.e., 'crowding in')
$k = 1$	zero (0%) crowding out
$0 > k > 1$	'partial' (0–100%) crowding out
$k = 0$	complete (100%) crowding out
$k < 0$	'super' (more than 100% crowding out)

Crowding out can be illustrated in the 45° line diagram. As noted in Chapter 6, this model assumes that investment is exogenously determined. This does not mean that investment is rigidly fixed, but rather that it is determined by factors outside the model. If the government runs a budget deficit, however, this requires the sale of government bonds and, to the extent that these sales have an effect on interest rates, there is likely to be a connection between government spending and investment which invalidates this assumption. There are two links in this chain.

First, there is the relationship between higher government borrowing and interest rates. Economic theory treats interest rates as the price which clears the money market, by moving to bring the demand for money into line with the supply. The demand for money has several dimensions: money is held for transactions and precautionary motives (which depends on the level of output and prices) and for speculative or savings motives (which depends on the opportunity cost of holding money, namely the interest rate). Extra government spending (unmatched by higher taxes) thus affects the money market in two ways. By tending to increase output, it increases the demand for transactions and precautionary balances, shifting the demand for money schedule to the right (see Figure 7.1a). At the same time, the sales of government securities necessary to finance this extra spending add to households' stock of financial wealth, increasing their demand for speculative balances at every rate of interest and reinforcing this rightward shift in the

FIGURE 7.1
(a) Equilibrium in the Money Market

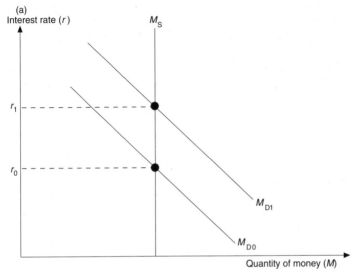

(b) Interest Rates and Investment

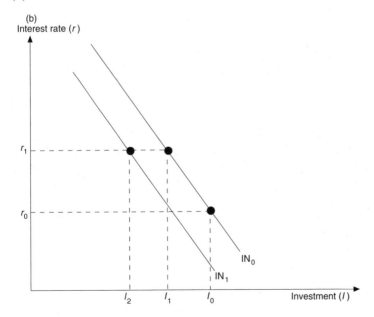

overall money demand schedule from M_{D0} to M_{D1}. The result is that, with an unchanged supply of money (M_s), the interest rate must rise from r_0 to r_1 to maintain equilibrium in the money market.

The second link in the chain is the relationship between interest rates and investment (see Figure 7.1b). The lower the interest rate, the larger the number of capital projects which will be profitable and the higher the level of corporate investment, and vice versa (see Chapter 8 for a more detailed discussion). Thus if deficit spending by the government increases interest rates from r_0 to r_1, the level of investment will fall from I_0 to I_1, leading to (partial) crowding out. Worse still, if the higher government spending were to undermine business confidence, shifting the investment schedule to the left from IN_0 to IN_1, it is possible that the induced fall in investment from I_0 to I_2 might actually *exceed* the increase in government spending, giving rise to super-crowding out. The net result of such crowding out (whether partial, complete or super) is a change in aggregate demand which is much less than the increased government spending might other-wise have been expected to produce (and possibly even negative, in the case of super-crowding out), due to the reduction of private sector invest-ment. Not only does crowding out reduce the effectiveness of activist fiscal policy as a means of controlling aggregate demand, but it also implies that such government spending is undertaken at the cost of lasting damage to the economy's long-run growth prospects.

Convinced by this analysis of the link between budget deficits and crowding out, the Conservative Government has followed a policy since 1979 of attempting to balance its budget over the medium term. The so-called 'Medium Term Financial Strategy' (MTFS) published annually since 1980, sets out annual targets for the budget deficit, which are designed to minimise the crowding out of productive investment (see Table 7.7); and, by implication, to minimise the negative impact of the budget balance on economic growth. This strategy of containing the budget deficit, which explicitly rejects the earlier Keynesian practice of deliberately creating budget deficits (or surpluses) as a means of fine-tuning aggregate demand, was generally achieved during the 1980s, although since the onset of the 1990–3 recession, the budget deficit has grown rapidly. Tax increases (although not in direct taxes) and spending cuts are planned for 1994 and beyond in order to restore the state's finances to balance in the medium term.

Synthesising the New Classical Debate

In terms of growth theories there are certainly alternatives, and in terms of their prescriptions for economic growth the New Classical economists, in

TABLE 7.7
Budget Deficit Targets and Outturns

Year	Target (% of GDP)	Outturn (% of GDP)
1979–80	4.50	4.8
1980–81	3.75	5.5
1981–82	4.25	3.5
1982–83	3.50	3.3
1983–84	2.75	3.3
1984–85	2.25	3.0
1985–86	2.00	1.5
1986–87	1.75	1.0
1987–88	1.00	−0.8
1988–89	−0.75	−3.0
1989–90	−2.75	−1.5
1990–91	1.25	−0.3
1991–92	1.25	2.4
1992–93	4.50	6.2

NOTE   A negative sign denotes a budget surplus
SOURCE   HM Treasury (1992) *Financial Statement and Budget Report 1992/93*, March, London.

contrast to the Keynesian school of thought, believe that free markets, left to their own devices, will best allocate resources between competing ends in an efficient way. They are sceptical of the Keynesian's insistence on stabilisation policy and the need for direct state intervention to promote growth. Indeed, New Classical economists typically regard attempts by the state to control private-sector activity as counterproductive, blaming Britain's relatively poor post-war growth record on excessive government interference via the process of crowding out. Inspired by this theoretical approach to economic growth, the post-1979 Conservative Government has directed policy at 'freeing the market' through various supply-side measures. Such approaches would include privatising nationalised industries, rationalising the tax and social security system, reforming Britain's notoriously inflexible labour market and attempting to curb budget deficits. Measuring the results of these changes is difficult, however. Powerful interest groups are loath to see their influence waning and the outcomes from such measures may only be seen in the medium to long term.

Capital Accumulation and Technological Progress 8

As noted in Chapter 5, investment in new products and processes (research and development) and in capital equipment is an essential prerequisite for sustained economic growth. This chapter examines Britain's record with regard to expenditure on research and development (R&D) and physical capital. It then explores the economic theory of investment in an attempt to identify the key factors that determine the level of investment and considers recent policies designed to stimulate private-sector investment against this theoretical background.

Britain's Record on Capital Investment

Figure 8.1 illustrates that, expressed as a percentage of GDP, capital investment in Britain falls well below the levels enjoyed in almost all of the other major economies. Table 8.1 shows that decomposing these depressing totals by sector reveals a rather mixed picture. Comparing 1990, the peak of the last boom, with 1979, the peak of the boom before that, it can be seen that some sectors, notably financial services and distribution, have seen a marked increase in their rates of investment. On the other hand, key manufacturing sectors like motor vehicles and mechanical engineering (sometimes regarded as the 'engines' of economic growth) experienced falls in the rate of investment over the 1980s. The divergent investment performance of different economic sectors throws into sharp relief the debate about whether or not manufacturing plays a special role in the growth process (see Chapter 3).

FIGURE 8.1
International Comparisons of Gross Fixed Capital Formation as a Proportion of GDP, 1979–90

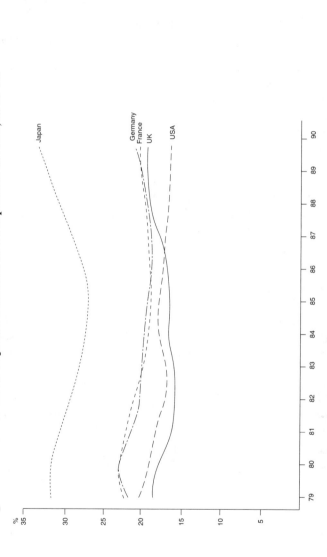

SOURCE   OECD (1992) *World Economic Outlook*, Paris.

TABLE 8.1
Investment and Capital Accumulation in Britain by Sector

Sector	Investment in 1990 (£bn, 1985 Prices)	Annual Average Growth of Gross Fixed Capital Stock (%)
Financial Services	9.68	313
Distribution	3.62	145
Communications	2.77	75
Construction	0.55	26
Chemicals	1.59	15
Motor Vehicles	0.86	–4
Energy	3.50	–10
Mech. Engineering	0.89	–23

SOURCE   DTI (1991) *Investment by Industry*, London.

Research and Development

Tables 8.2 and 8.3 illustrate Britain's recent record on R&D. Table 8.2 shows that the proportion of GDP devoted to total R&D is somewhat lower in Britain than in the United States, Germany and Japan. Moreover, while all the other major trading nations increased the share of GDP devoted to R&D in the 1980s, in Britain the ratio remained static.

TABLE 8.2
R&D Expenditure (% of GDP)

Country	1970	1979	1989
Britain	2.2	2.2	2.2
France	1.9	1.8	2.3
Germany	2.1	2.4	2.9
Italy	0.9	0.9	1.3
Japan	1.9	2.2	3.0
United States	2.7	2.4	2.8

SOURCE   OECD (1990) *Main Science and Technology Indicators*, Paris.

Table 8.3 offers an international comparison of gross spending on R&D and output in terms of registered international patents (licences granted to the inventors of new products or processes to protect them from imitation). It shows that, although R&D resources appear to have been efficiently used in Britain – the average dollar cost per patent is somewhat lower for Britain than most of the other countries listed – Britain spends the least and (with the exception of France) registers the fewest patents of the five advanced industrial economies.

TABLE 8.3
R&D Expenditure and Patent Registrations (1989)

Country	Gross R&D Expenditure ($bn)	Business R&D Expenditure ($bn)	Registered International Patents ('000s)
Britain	17.0	11.3	63.4
Germany	26.7	19.5	137.1
France	19.0	11.4	56.1
Japan	58.0	40.4	115.0
United States	144.8	101.6	239.8

SOURCE   OECD (1990) *Main Science and Technology Indicators*, Paris.

The Decision to Invest

For private companies, the decision to invest – whether in physical plant and equipment or in R&D – is motivated by the expectation that the project concerned will generate future net revenues that exceed the initial capital cost. For example, the Channel tunnel linking Britain and France was under construction for several years at a cost of billions of pounds. Not until the tunnel finally opened in 1994 was the operating company able to begin earning revenue to set against these massive capital costs. For years into the future, however, the tunnel will generate net revenues (i.e., gross revenues net of operating costs), so that over its planned lifetime it should produce a substantial profit.

The example of the Channel tunnel illustrates another important point about the process of commercial investment appraisal. Because the returns from investments do not normally accrue until some point into the future, companies must take into account the opportunity cost of the capital they have tied up in the project when comparing the costs with the expected net revenues. To take a simple example, a project with a capital cost of £100 which provides a one-off net revenue of £105 after twelve months appears superficially attractive, yielding an apparent 'profit' of £5 (or a return on investment of 5 per cent). But suppose the rate of interest (i.e., the opportunity cost of capital) is 10 per cent. If the firm had borrowed the capital (£100) it needed, at the end of the twelve month project, it would have had to repay not £100, but £110 (£100 × 110 per cent). Since the return from the project is only £105, the firm would have made a loss of £5 (i.e., after deducting the rate of interest, the return on investment would have been –5 per cent, rather than 5 per cent as before). Similarly, if the firm had financed the project with its own capital, it would have to deduct from the net revenue of £105 not just the £100 capital cost, but also the £10 (£100 × 10 per cent) that it could have earned by holding interest-bearing financial assets instead. Again, instead of a £5 profit, the firm would be looking at a £5 loss.

Given the importance of time, the only way to make a meaningful comparison of capital costs and future net revenues is to adjust the latter to allow for the opportunity cost of capital. In general terms £1 in one year's time is equivalent to £1/(1+r) today, in the sense that £1 invested today at an interest rate, r, would yield a total return of £1(1+r) in one year's time; or alternatively, £1 borrowed today at an interest rate, r, would oblige the borrower to repay £1(1+r) in one year's time. Using a simple example may clear up any difficulties. If the rate of interest is 10 per cent and I have £100 to invest, then next year the £100 will be worth £110. Keeping the rate of interest at 10 per cent, suppose I know that next year I will receive £110, how much would this be worth now? Anyone with any sense would only give me at the most £100. If they gave me more, say £105, then I could invest this at the current interest rate of 10 per cent and receive £115.50 in a year's time. If I was given £100 now and chose to invest this at 10 per cent then it would give me the £110 next year. By the same logic, £1 in two year's time is equivalent to £1/(1+r)(1+r) or, more simply, £1/(1+r)². (Note that in this approach, the interest rate, r, is expressed as a decimal rather than a percentage; e.g., 0.1 rather than 10 per cent.) Calculating the profit from a project in terms of today's money (the 'net present value' or NPV) thus involves summing the adjusted future net revenues and subtracting the capital costs of the project. The relationship between the net present value, future net revenues (R), capital cost (C) and the rate of interest (r) is given in the following equation, where i is the number of years from the start of the project:

$$\text{NPV} = \sum \frac{(R)^i}{(1+r)^i} - C$$

For example, in the simple example given above of a project with a capital cost of £100, a net revenue of £105 after one year and an interest rate of 10 per cent (i.e., 0.1), the net present value would be:

$$\text{NPV} = \sum \frac{(105)}{(1+0.1)^1} - 100$$
$$= 95.45 - 100$$
$$= -4.55$$

where the net present value of £4.55 is simply the present value of the £5 loss discussed above; that is, £5/(1 + 0.1). Only if the net present value is positive, so that the sum of the adjusted (or 'discounted') future net revenues exceeds the capital cost will the project be commercially viable.

This brief review of the mechanics of investment appraisal can be used to illustrate the key influences on private-sector investment, namely:

1. the capital cost of the project;
2. the expected net revenue in the future;
3. the rate of interest.

Ceteris paribus, the lower 1 and the higher 2 and 3, the greater the number of investment projects that will be commercially viable.

The Role of Taxation and Subsidies

The analysis above abstracts from the effect of taxation and subsidies on the capital cost of the project and the net revenues from the point of the investing company. What ultimately matters to corporate decision-makers is not the total capital cost of the project, nor the total (discounted) net revenues it generates, but those costs and revenues which are respectively borne and received by the company. It is the difference between these totals that will impact on its earnings (i.e., gross profits net of interest, taxes and subsidies). For example, to the extent that the firm receives a subsidy towards the capital cost of the project, the effective value of C in the equation above will be lower; conversely, taxes (e.g., VAT, employers' national insurance contributions, etc.) reduce the effective value of R over time.

Of the two distortions, subsidies are the more interesting, since they have been historically employed by governments with the express purpose of promoting investment. Corporate tax systems, on the other hand, are for the most part designed to minimise their impact on commercial decision-making (e.g., corporation tax is levied on gross profits, so should not in principle alter profit-maximising behaviour). As already noted, subsidies may take the form of an investment grant, which directly reduces the capital cost of the project. Alternatively, the subsidy may be a tax allowance, which allows the company to offset the cost of the project against its future liability for corporation tax. In analytical terms, tax allowances are broadly equivalent to investment grants, in the sense that they both reduce the effective cost of the project to the investing company.

The Importance of Risk

Investment appraisal necessarily involves taking a view about the future. Even the capital cost of a project may not be known with certainty, especially if it may take several years to complete. And normally the likely net revenues which will flow from the project cannot be known precisely. Operating costs may vary unpredictably. Future revenue flows may be above or below the company's projections: perhaps a new substitute product will be developed, resulting in a slump in demand; perhaps new competitors will enter the market, driving down prices; perhaps there will be an expected boom or slump, playing havoc with the company's sales forecasts. Both operating costs and revenues may be especially prone to fluctuations in exchange rates, since almost every company relies on imported inputs (e.g., energy, raw materials, intermediate products) and most compete with foreign companies, whether in the British or overseas markets.

The presence of 'risk' injects an additional dimension into the process of investment appraisal. In practice, the figures that are entered into the calculation for C and R are not known magnitudes, but rather the company's 'best guess'. In the event, the actual outturns may prove to be higher or lower than this estimate. This begs an important question: in the real world, is it realistic to base decisions on, say, an expected net return of £100, when the actual figure may turn out to be anywhere between £0 and £200? For example, most people, when asked whether they would rather have £100 straight away or first gamble it on the toss of a coin (when they would get back either £0 or £200), choose the safe alternative. In other words, they are risk-averse. They may need an expected return (the profit multiplied by the probability of success) to be, say, £120 before they would be prepared to risk losing a certain £100.

It must be possible, therefore, to map out all the possible investments between which an investor is indifferent. Some of these combinations will be investments which are very certain but may give a low rate of return whilst others are more risky, and to compensate for this risk a higher rate of return would be expected. If an investor is indifferent between two investments, one with a low rate of return which is certain, and the other with a high rate of return, but which is more risky, then both would be placed on the same indifference curve. Figure 8.2 illustrates an in-

FIGURE 8.2
Trade-off Between Risk and Expected Return

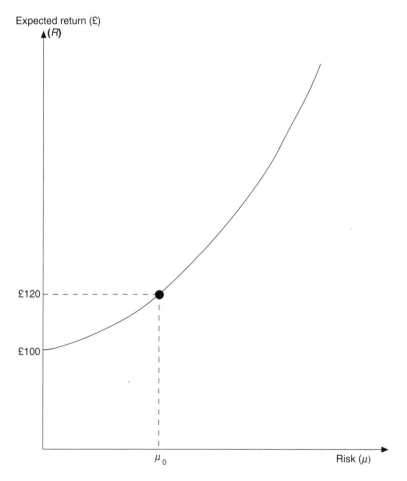

difference curve relating expected return to risk (i.e., the variability of the return) for a risk-averse investor. While everyone knows gamblers who, by definition, are risk-lovers (they are prepared to play games like roulette in which the expected return is less than the size of the bet), such behaviour is regarded as irresponsible to the point of social unacceptability once bets become sufficiently large that losing endangers the standard of living of the gambler and his or her family. For most corporate investments, where a major unsuccessful project may result in liquidation (e.g., as Sinclair found with its innovative, but ill-fated, electric-powered tricycle), strong risk aversion is the norm.

Figure 8.2 illustrates the important principle of 'certainty equivalence' outlined above. It shows that, for the individual concerned, the investor is indifferent between a certain £100 (i.e., £100 with zero risk) and the prospect of an expected return of £120 with a risk of μ_0 (where μ_0 may be, for example, ± £10). The indifference curve simply shows the expected return necessary to compensate the investor for ever higher levels of risk. The significance of this principle for investment appraisal is that, for a risk-averse investor, the relevant value of R is not the expected net return, regardless of risk, but rather its certainty equivalent. It is for this reason that shares in risky, innovative high-tech companies typically offer so much higher expected returns than investments in reliable, well-established 'blue-chip' corporations. The higher the perceived risk, the lower the certainty equivalent of its expected return and the lower the net present value.

The concept of risk (and risk aversion) explains why many private-sector companies are loath to invest in speculative R&D and innovative new products and processes. Although the expected net returns may be very high, the costs of failure may run to bankruptcy. The result is a tendency to avoid the risky – and potentially most profitable – investments. In the business world, there used to be an adage which sums up this attitude: 'no one ever got fired for buying IBM'. While IBM's computers were historically far more expensive than its competitors, they were exceptionally reliable. Although the capital cost ate into the purchasing company's profits, at least it could be sure that its computer systems were secure from a damaging malfunction. In contrast, IBM's competitors offered much cheaper machines, but the purchaser ran the risk that a bargain buy might break down and cost its business millions of dollars in lost orders.

Policies to Promote Investment

The review of the investment appraisal process above suggests a raft of measures which governments might employ to promote investment.

Recalling the linchpin equation linking capital costs, expected net revenues, and the interest rate,

$$\text{NPV} = \sum \frac{(R)^i}{(1+r)^i} - C$$

and taking into account the qualifications outlined above, the main influences on investment over which the government can (or could) exert control are:

1. the rate of interest;
2. subsidies for capital investment (whether in the form of investment grants or capital allowances against tax);
3. taxes on, or linked to, net revenues and other government-imposed costs of production (e.g., employers' National Insurance Contributions (NICs), statutory sickness and maternity benefits, etc.);
4. the stability (or riskiness) of the political and financial environment.

Interest Rates

Economists typically draw an important distinction between the 'real interest rate' and the 'nominal interest rate', arguing that it is the real interest rate that matters for investment decisions. The real interest rate (r_r) is simply the nominal, or actual, interest rate (r) less the rate of inflation $(\dot{P})$:

$$r_r = r - \dot{P}$$

Even though the nominal interest rate may appear high (and discouraging to investment), to the extent that there is also high inflation, the money value of future net revenues will be increased as a result of the rise in the general price level. What matters for the investment decision, therefore, is the level of nominal interest rates relative to the rate of inflation, and it is this which is given by the real interest rate. A low (or negative) real interest rate implies that, relative to inflation, nominal interest rates are low; that is, inflation will boost future net revenues by more than the nominal interest rate will discount them, giving rise to a higher net present value than when the real interest rate is high. Table 8.4 shows that, measured in this way, the environment for investment has worsened considerably since the 1970s, with a rise in real interest rates in most developed countries, including Britain.

However, it is worth pointing out that, for risk-averse companies, high nominal interest rates may of themselves exert a separate, inhibiting effect

TABLE 8.4
Real Interest Rates (%)

Country	1971–5	1976–80	1981–5	1986–90
Britain	−1.6	−1.1	4.7	3.9
France	−0.2	−0.4	4.1	6.1
Germany	2.7	3.1	4.5	5.4
Italy	−2.6	−2.3	3.4	4.8

SOURCE   Adapted from *Eurostat*, various editions, HMSO, London.

on investment, even though real rates may be low. The reason is that, when nominal interest rates are high, the cash flows out of the firm are high and this may be regarded as a problem in its own right, regardless of the overall net present value of the project. For example, imagine two economies, A and B, in which nominal interest rates are 5 per cent and 20 per cent, and inflation rates 0 per cent and 20 per cent, respectively. Country B appears to be the more attractive for investment, since the real interest rate is 0 per cent, as opposed to 5 per cent in A. However, consider the cash outflows necessary to service a £100 loan in each country. For a firm in country A, it has to pay out only £5 per annum; for a firm in country B, its debt service cost is £20. For the former firm, variability in its cash earnings year-on-year will present far fewer problems than for the latter, which will suffer a negative cash outflow should its earnings dip below £20.

Home-buyers in Britain are acutely aware of this phenomenon. When inflation rose sharply in 1988–9, nominal interest rates followed suit. While the real interest rate actually rose relatively little in 1988–90, the massive increase in monthly cash payments associated with the higher nominal interest rates caused serious difficulties for many home-buyers and the number of repossessions soared. Partly for this reason, the Conservative Government has laid great importance on the need to achieve low, stable inflation and so low nominal interest rates. However, as Table 8.5 shows, its record to date has been disappointing, particulary in comparison with other EC countries.

Investment Subsidies

State subsidies for industry are normally designed to reduce the effective cost to an investing firm of the initial capital cost of a project, increasing

Table 8.5
Comparative Inflation Records (1979–92)

Country	Average Annual Inflation Rate (%)
Britain	7.3
France	6.6
Germany	2.2
Italy	9.4

SOURCE   Commission for the European Communities, *General Reports on the Activities of the European Community, European Economy,* various, Brussels.

its net present value – and hence its attractiveness. Historically, British governments used widespread investment subsidies (or grants) in an effort to promote investment and industrial restructuring. However, the Conservative Government has been generally less enthusiastic about this policy tool. The main disadvantage of such subsidies, widely criticised by New Classical economists, is that it distorts investment decisions in favour of those projects favoured by the government. The result is that the government may find itself wasting taxpayers' money by encouraging investment in sectors and industries which would not otherwise be viable without the assistance. Rather than accelerating economic growth, such subsidies may simply prop up ailing, and ultimately doomed, 'lame ducks'. The investment grants to steel and shipbuilding during the 1960s and 1970s are a good case in point. A second, related shortcoming of investment subsidies is that, if other governments are doing the same thing, they may simply cancel each other out. Table 8.6 illustrates the scale of state subsidies to industry in other major advanced economies. For example, if one country gives investment subsidies to its own national producer, it should in principle succeed in establishing that firm as a market leader, allowing it to export into other markets. But if all other governments do the same, the overseas markets for the investments will not be there. Worse still, even if each government believes that the others will subsidise investment in leading-edge technologies like telecommunications, aerospace, etc., it will still choose to subsidise investment by its own producers to ensure that it does not fall behind. The result of this non-co-operative behaviour is that governments may collectively waste resources, encouraging over-investment, and hence chronic over-capacity, in industries they deem (often wrongly) to be of strategic value in the global growth race.

TABLE 8.6
Average State Subsidies to Industry (% of GDP)

Country	1973–9	1985–9
Britain	2.7	1.7
France	2.5	3.0
Germany	2.1	2.2
Italy	3.2	3.3
United States	0.4	0.7

SOURCE   Crafts, N. (1992) 'Productivity Growth Reconsidered', *Economic Policy*, vol. 15 (Oct).

The phenomenon of individual governments each rationally pursuing a course of action which leads to a collective outcome that no one wants is an example of the so-called 'prisoners' dilemma' (see Table 8.7). The prisoners' dilemma is normally illustrated by the case of two criminals, who have been arrested while speeding from the scene of a bank robbery. The police have insufficient evidence to charge them for the robbery in the absence of a confession, but could secure a conviction for reckless driving and resisting arrest. The criminals are taken to separate cells and both offered the same choice by the police: if neither confesses, both will be convicted to five years in prison for the driving offences; if only one confesses, he will be freed, but the other will be prosecuted on the basis of this confession and sentenced to 20 years; finally, if both confess, each will get a slightly less severe sentence of 15 years for the bank robbery. What is each criminal to do? If criminal B stays silent, then A's best course of action is clearly to confess and avoid prison. If B confesses, then

TABLE 8.7
The Prisoners' Dilemma

Prisoner A	Prisoner B	
	Confess	Do Not Confess
Confess	15, 15	0, 20
Do Not Confess	20, 0	5, 5

NOTE   The numbers represent the number of years served by each prisoner (A, B).

A should also confess, since by staying silent A will be sentenced to 20, rather than 15, years. So regardless of what he thinks B will do, A will always confess. And since the situation is symmetrical, B will always confess as well. The result of this dilemma is that, while they would agree to stay silent and serve only five years in prison if they could communicate and reach a co-operative decision, when they act independently they quite rationally choose a collectively sub-optimal outcome in which they both end up serving 15 years.

The only solution to a prisoners' dilemma is to collectively agree to the optimal solution. In the case of state subsidies for investment, this means agreeing not to provide government finance to industry at below market interest rates. The European Community has been particulary keen to standardise and limit 'state aids' under the 1992 initiative to 'complete the internal market'. Predictably, however, it has had least success when it has come to dealing with the subsidies that member governments give to attract foreign companies (e.g., Japanese car producers like Nissan and Toyota), which governments fear will go elsewhere unless they can be bribed with sufficiently tempting 'carrots'.

Corporate Taxation

While the Conservative Government has been strongly critical of invest-ment subsidies, which it regards as distorting commercial investment decisions, it has taken the view that investment is best served by a low rate of corporate tax on profits, which maximises the expected, post-tax return from capital projects. Table 8.8 summarises the main changes in corporate taxes since 1979. As a result of these changes, by the end of the 1980s, British corporate tax rates were amongst the lowest of the advanced indus-trial economies (see Table 8.9).

Macroeconomic Stability

As noted in Chapter 6, the British economy has been subject to a rela-tively high degree of instability at the macroeconomic level. The business cycle, and the fluctuations in output, inflation and nominal interest rates, have typically been more pronounced in Britain than in the other major industrial nations and this is widely regarded as a partial cause of Britain's low investment and growth rates. There is, moreover, some reason to believe that British governments, rather than simply failing to limit the scale of this volatility, have actually been responsible for the degree of macroeconomic instability. It is notable that Germany and Japan, which have enjoyed a relatively stable macroeconomic climate, differ from

TABLE 8.8
Main Tax Changes Affecting Companies since 1979

1984 Budget
- main rate of Corporation Tax to be reduced in stages from 52 per cent to 35 per cent by the end of 1986–7;
- phasing out of initial allowances of 100 per cent for plant and machinery and of 75 per cent for industrial buildings by 1986–7;
- abolition with immediate effect (i.e. from 13 March 1984) of stock relief.

1991 Budget
- main rate of Corporation Tax on profits earned in 1990–1 reduced from 35 to 34 per cent;
- main rate of corporation tax to be further reduced to 33 per cent on profits earned in 1991–2.

SOURCE   HM Treasury (1991), Financial Statement and Budget Reports, various, London.

TABLE 8.9
Corporate Tax Rates on Profit (%)

Country	1979	1990
Britain	52	35
France	50	42
Germany	56	56
Italy	36	47
Japan	55	56
United States	51	40

SOURCE   OECD (1991) *Corporate Tax Harmonisation*, OECD, Paris.

Britain in important ways. In Japan, the Liberal Democratic Party has been in power continuously for three decades. In Germany, monetary policy is under the control of an independent central bank, the *Bundesbank*, which is charged with responsibility for ensuring price stability.

In both countries, although for different reasons, their governments have not engaged in the deliberate manipulation of aggregate demand for political ends (e.g., increasing aggregate demand and generating boom conditions in advance of an election in order to improve their prospects of regaining power): successive Japanese governments have not needed to, because the opposition parties are so weak; while in Germany, power over the main arm of demand management policy, namely monetary policy, has long been in the hands of an independent central bank. In Britain, in contrast, successive governments (both Labour and Conservative) have repeatedly succumbed to the temptation to engineer a pre-election boom, imposing unnecessarily large fluctuations in output and demand on the business sector as a direct consequence. The pre-election boom in 1987, since dubbed the 'Lawson boom' after the Chancellor who presided over it, and the subsequent deep recession in the early 1990s, stands as a particularly egregious example of a 'political business cycle'. Despite Conservative protestations about their commitment to low, stable inflation, many commentators believe that only by following the German example, and transferring responsibility for monetary policy to a constitutionally independent Bank of England, will Britain be able to match the macroeconomic stability of its two most successful competitors.

Investment and the Capital Market

The continuing failure of British firms to invest as heavily as their overseas rivals, despite the removal of allegedly restrictive taxes and government regulations, suggests that there may be inherent deficiencies in the way the private sector functions. For example, critics of recent policy point to the structure of the British capital market, which – in contrast to those in Germany and Japan – allows companies that do not maximise short-term profits to be taken over against their will. As a result, British management may be deterred from undertaking the investment essential for longer-term economic success, since payback periods (i.e., the number of years taken for cumulative net revenues to exceed the initial capital cost) are typically lengthy; as a result, investment reduces profits in the short term, making investing companies liable to takeover. Table 8.10 shows that the number of companies publicly quoted on the stock market in Britain is much higher than in all other advanced economies except the United States. However, it also highlights the fact that unquoted companies may also be taken over, although outside Britain and the United States most takeovers are not hostile in nature.

The role of the capital market (i.e., the Stock Exchange) in engendering a 'short-termist', anti-investment attitude amongst British managers is highly controversial. While many commentators blame City myopia for holding back long-term investment in Britain, others argue that the capital

TABLE 8.10
Quoted Companies and Takeovers, 1990

Country	Number of Quoted Companies	Number of Takeovers
Britain	2569	1524
France	678	1967
Germany	742	1342
Italy	211	47
Japan	173	1100
United States	5585	2647

Sources *Translink's 1992 The Merger and Acquisitions Monthly,* various editions; European Commission (1991) *Panorama of Europe,* Brussels.

markets discipline managements into using resources most effectively. Companies which failed to exploit profitable investment opportunities would, they point out, have a lower anticipated flow of future profits – and hence a lower share price – than would otherwise be the case. Identifying this weakness, rivals would seek to take over such companies, since by buying their assets at a low price and then undertaking the investment with a new management in place, the buyers would see the market valuation of their acquisitions rise. Indeed, so convinced is the Government of the capital market's ability to ensure the best use of resources by management that it regularly cites this power as the main route to greater economic efficiency within privatised enterprises (see Chapter 7).

Getting the Investment Climate Right

Britain's record on capital investment and R&D relative to other major industrial nations appears to be weak. It could be suggested that one factor to blame for this is that the economic conditions have not been consistent or appropriate to encourage investment behaviour, but other factors, such as interest rates (real and nominal), the availability and scale of investment subsidies, the structure and level of corporate profits tax, appear to be equally as important as the stability of the macroeconomic environment. With the exception of investment subsidies, which the Conservative Government has rejected on the grounds that they distort commercial investment decisions, recent years have seen concerted policy measures designed to improve the climate for investment. However, continuing high inflation in Britain (together with high nominal interest rates) and the Government's apparent unwillingness to eschew the use of the political business cycle for political ends, means that British companies still face a less attractive climate for investment than their main international rivals. The cumulative effect of this has reduced one of the engines of the growth process.

Labour Market Flexibility and Human Capital

9

Chapter 5 showed that changes in the quantity and the quality of the labour force both have an important impact on economic growth. This chapter explores the role of the labour market, and the part played by the trade union movement, in promoting economic growth and structural change and reviews the recent policies that have been used in this area.

Aggregate Supply and the Labour Market

Chapter 5 highlighted how increases in the quantity of labour shift the supply schedule in Figure 9.1c to the right, from L_{s0} to L_{s1}, increasing equilibrium employment and shifting the long-run aggregate supply schedule to the right from $LRAS_0$ to $LRAS_1$ (and the natural rate of output from Y_0 to Y_1). In recent years, various policies have been directed at increasing the supply of labour, notably tax and social security reforms, as well as legislation to control the activity of trade unions, which are accused of restricting labour supply in order to achieve higher wages.

Increases in the quality, or productivity, of labour, on the other hand, initially affect the aggregate production function in Figure 9.1b, shifting it upwards from APF_0 to APF_1. Since the demand for labour (i.e., the marginal revenue product) schedule in Figure 9.1c is derived directly from the aggregate production function, an increase in labour productivity shifts the demand for labour schedule to the right, in this case from MRP_0 to MRP_1. Taken together, and given the original labour supply schedule, L_{s0}, the two effects combine to shift the long-run aggregate supply schedule from $LRAS_0$ to $LRAS_1$. Various government initiatives to promote education and

FIGURE 9.1

(a) Shifts in the Long-run Aggregate Supply Curve

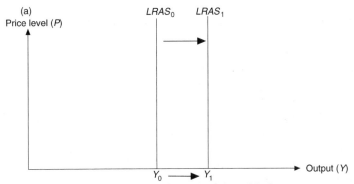

(b) Improvements in the Quality/Productivity of Labour

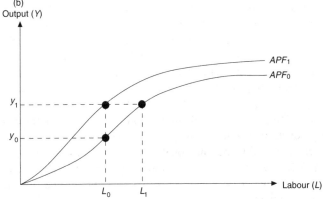

(c) The Impact of an Increase in the Quality of Labour

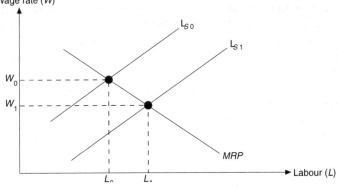

training have been inspired by the need to improve the quality of British labour.

Trade Unions, Structural Change and Economic Growth

There are several ways in which trade unions may, in principle, inhibit growth and structural change. For example, the trade union movement in Britain has historically been 'craft-based', with workers joining unions that cover their particular occupation (e.g., printing or engineering). The monopoly power of an individual trade union thus resides in its power to control labour of a specific functional type. For example, a nationally based engineering union can bargain with employers from a very powerful base, since companies will find it very difficult to recruit qualified engineering workers who are not union members.

One potential disadvantage of this union structure in Britain is that it may militate against supply-side change. R&D and investment strengthen the economy by improving productivity; that is, by changing the way people work in ways that increase output per head. For example, the computerisation of newspaper typesetting, which allows journalists to type their stories into a computer that automatically sets up the printing presses, was a great advance over the old system, which required print workers to manually assemble plates of individual letters from the journalists' draft typescript. This technological innovation dramatically improved both labour productivity and technical quality in the newspaper industry, but by fundamentally altering the functional nature of the jobs involved, its introduction proved very disruptive, culminating in the protracted and bitter 'Wapping' dispute between the print workers' union and the Murdoch newspaper company.

Part of the difficulty stemmed from the fact that the computerisation of the print-setting operation in the newspaper business transformed what had been a manual job done by skilled print workers – represented by their own craft union – into a job which could be done directly by journalists, supported by electrical engineers to maintain the new equipment. The print workers' union was thus bound to defend the position of its members against the effects of the changes which, given the intransigence of the employer concerned, resulted in prolonged strike action. The Conservative Government's argument is, therefore, that since economic growth necessarily involves continuously redefining workers' jobs and functional responsibilities, old craft-based trade unions which have a duty to protect the jobs of their membership from structural change inhibit R&D and investment in new products and processes.

Other Obstacles to Labour Market Flexibility

There may, however, be other obstacles to structural change and economic growth at work. Note that Figures 9.1a–9.1c are 'static equilibrium' models; i.e., they illustrate the stationary points of equilibrium, to which the economy will tend. To the extent that there are various obstacles to the free functioning of markets, however, these equilibria may never actually be achieved, so that the 'effective' supply of labour – and hence the actual quantity of goods and services supplied – is lower than Figure 9.1c would suggest.

One manifestation of a reduction in the effective labour supply would be a rise in the 'natural rate of unemployment', and this phenomenon has indeed been observed in a number of advanced economies over the last 20 years (see Table 9.1). The natural rate of unemployment is the rate consistent with equilibrium in the labour market; that is, with the supply of labour equal to the demand for labour. But if supply equals demand, how can there be any unemployment? In the real world, of course, the answer depends upon the way in which the government chooses to officially record unemployment. When the labour market is in equilibrium, there are millions of adults who, for whatever reason, choose not to seek work at the equilibrium wage rate. Are they unemployed? For example, is a trained solicitor who looks after her children at home unemployed? Is a male accountant who takes early retirement at 50 unemployed? In principle, although neither wants a job at the going wage rate, each may begin looking (and regard her- or himself as unemployed) if wages were higher, Clearly, the actual definition of unemployment is problematic.

TABLE 9.1
The Natural Rate of Unemployment (%)

Country	1971–6	1977–82	1983–7
Britain	2.2	4.6	7.4
Germany	1.1	3.1	6.0
Italy	7.6	7.0	7.3
United States	5.4	5.7	6.0

SOURCE   Burda, M. and Wyplosz, C. (1993) *Macroeconomics: A European Text* (London: Oxford University Press); Minford, P. (1993). *The Costs of Europe* (Manchester: Manchester University Press).

However, in terms of our simple labour supply and demand model (see Figure 9.1c above), our definition of the natural rate of unemployment excludes workers who are 'voluntarily' unemployed. It refers to those workers who, in equilibrium, are simply moving between jobs; that is, leaving one job to go to another. Equilibrium in the labour market means that the quantity of jobs being offered by employers (i.e., actual jobs filled plus unfilled vacancies) equals the quantity of jobs demanded by workers (i.e., jobs taken plus unemployed seeking jobs). Labour market equilibrium is thus consistent with the idea of some minimum level of unemployment, as workers leave one job and go to another. As they move, they fill one vacancy and, in moving, create another. If the workforce is 25 million and each person takes one week to move jobs once a year, then on average, at any moment in time, 0.5 million people will be temporarily unemployed even though the labour market overall is in full equilibrium.

It follows that the more difficult it is for people to move smoothly between jobs, either because their skills do not match precisely the jobs on offer or because they live in a different part of the country from the location of the new jobs, the longer are workers temporarily unemployed while switching jobs. If, in our example, each worker was unemployed for four weeks, there would on average be 2 million unemployed at any moment in time. In Britain, the pace of structural change in the economy is so rapid (see Chapter 2), with manufacturing shedding labour faster than the expanding service sector can take up the slack, that the number of unemployed consistent with labour market equilibrium (i.e., the natural rate of unemployment) rose in the 1970s and early 1980s. The Government has accordingly laid great emphasis on the need to promote greater labour market flexibility, in an effort to bring down the natural rate of unemployment.

Trade Union Legislation

Since 1979, a series of statutes has placed restrictions on trade union activity, in order, according to a Treasury statement in 1986, to:

> *'reduce the monopoly power of the trade unions ... [and so] create a climate in which realistic pay bargaining and acceptance of flexible working practices become the norm'* (*Economic Progress Report: A More Flexible Labour Market*, Jan–Feb, 1986)

The Conservative Government has targeted two aspects of trades unions in particular: first, their ability to undertake strike action, which has historically been protected from normal laws of contract by specific legislation (i.e., an employer is entitled to sue an individual worker who withdraws his or her labour for breach of contract, but a trade union is legally immune from such sanctions when it takes industrial action); and secondly, their right to enforce a 'closed shop' (an arrangement whereby all employees within a company must belong to a recognised trade union).

With regard to strikes and other forms of industrial action, the legislation has gradually restricted the circumstances in which trades unions are entitled to immunity from prosecution by companies adversely affected by their actions. The 1980 Employment Act, for example, restricted picketing to an individual's place of employment, thereby making secondary picketing unlawful. Consequently, strikers picketing at locations other than their own workplace are now liable to civil action for interfering with employment or commercial contracts. The 1980 Act also restricted the legality of other forms of secondary industrial action, such as the 'blacking' of goods; action must be confined to a direct customer or supplier of the employer with whom the union is in dispute.

The 1982 Employment Act tightened up the definition of a 'trade dispute' (i.e., industrial action immune from civil action). It specified that a trade dispute must be between workers and their employer. Furthermore, it required that a trade dispute must 'wholly or mainly' relate to employment matters, preventing unions from mounting the sort of political strikes which had enabled the miners to affect severely industrial production in the early 1970s. The 1982 Act also enabled trade unions to be sued in their own names, so that union funds were placed directly at risk. It laid down that a union would be liable for unlawful industrial action authorised or endorsed by a responsible person from the union concerned, although limits were placed on the damages courts could award.

The 1984 Trade Union Act restricted a union's immunity to cases in which industrial action has been formally approved in advance by the union members concerned. It provided that a union would lose its immunity unless it had first obtained majority support from its members – via a secret ballot – before authorising, or endorsing, industrial action. This was followed by the 1988 Employment Act, which gave union members the right to apply for a court order restraining their union from organising industrial action in the absence of a ballot approving such action. The 1988 Act also prohibited unions from disciplining their members for failing to take part in industrial action.

A second dimension to legislation relating to trade unions concerned statutory support for the closed shop, which was gradually removed during the 1980s. The 1980 Employment Act extended the grounds on which employees could object to union membership and tried to protect existing employees when a closed shop was introduced. It became unfair for an employer to dismiss staff for nonmembership of a union, provided they could show they had conscientious or deeply held personal reasons for not wishing to join or had been engaged before a closed shop agreement was concluded. The 1980 Act also attempted to ensure that future closed shops would only come into existence with the overwhelming support of the employees affected. It stipulated that if any new closed shop agreement was not approved of by at least 80 per cent of those to be covered by it, it would be unfair for the employer concerned to dismiss anyone for not being a union member.

The 1982 Employment Act sought to encourage periodic reviews of existing closed shops. It made it unfair for an employer to dismiss anyone for nonmembership of a union, unless a closed shop agreement had been supported by 80 per cent of affected employees in a secret ballot within the previous five years. The 1982 Act also substantially increased the level of compensation payable to those unfairly dismissed in a closed shop situation. The 1988 Employment Act gave increased protection to employers and employees against the operation of closed shops. It repealed the earlier provisions that had permitted dismissal for nonmembership of a union where an 'approved' closed shop was in operation, thereby making dismissal for nonmembership of a union automatically unfair. It also removed all legal immunity for industrial action taken by a union to force an employer to create or maintain any sort of closed shop practice.

The 1990 Employment Act made it unlawful for employers to deny applicants a job because they were not union members. The 1990 Act also outlawed all secondary industrial action by making a union legally liable when it takes action against any customer or supplier of the employer with whom it is in dispute. In addition, the Act made unions legally responsible for unofficial strikes called by shop stewards or any lay officer – when industrial action is organised by any union official (fulltime or parttime), the action will either have to be put to the test of a secret ballot or be repudiated in writing by the union concerned. Finally, the Act enabled employers to selectively dismiss workers taking unofficial industrial action.

The results of this legislative onslaught on the trade union movement have been profound. Although it is difficult to disentangle the effects of the new laws (which have tended to reduce the benefits of union membership) from those resulting from structural economic change (which have altered the composition of the employed labour force, creating female, part-time jobs at the expense of traditional, full-time manual employment), the fact remains that between 1979 and 1992, union density fell slightly (see Table 9.2). Although the Conservative Government has never suggested that it actively sought this outcome, the decline in union membership has nevertheless been at least partially influenced by the more hostile legislative environment and has played a major part in altering the balance of power in the industrial relations arena.

TABLE 9.2
Trade Union Density (Proportion of Employed Labour Force Belonging to a Trade Union)

Country	1970	1988
Britain	44.8	41.5
France	22.3	12.0
Germany	33.0	33.8
Italy	36.9	39.6
United States	22.8	16.4

SOURCE   Burda, M. and Wyplosz, C. (1993), *Macroeconomics: A European Text* (London: Oxford University Press).

A less controversial indicator of the success of the Government's new legal framework for wage bargaining has been the marked fall in the number of days lost through industrial disputes. Although there was a sudden surge in days lost during the protracted and highly divisive miners'

TABLE 9.3
Strike Activity in Britain

Year	Recorded Strikes	Workers on Strike (millions)	Working Days Lost (millions)	Working Days Lost per 1000 Workers
1979	2.1	4.6	29.5	1,273
1980	1.3	0.8	12.0	521
1981	1.3	1.5	4.3	195
1982	1.5	2.1	5.3	248
1983	1.4	0.6	3.8	178
1984	1.2	1.5	27.1	1,278
1985	0.9	0.8	6.4	299
1986	1.1	0.7	1.9	90
1987	1.0	0.9	3.5	164
1988	0.8	0.8	3.7	166
1989	0.7	0.7	4.1	182
1990	0.6	0.3	1.9	83

SOURCE   *Employment Gazette*, various.

strike of 1984–5, the underlying trend since 1979 appears to have been firmly downwards.

The Effect of Taxes and Social Security on Labour Supply

The effect of taxes and social security on the incentive to work is best analysed using the simple tools of microeconomics. The important point in analysing the supply of labour is to recognise that the decision by a worker to supply work is equivalent to the decision to give up leisure. Thus, the appropriate analysis is to consider the choice between income and leisure – every hour of leisure taken is an hour of income sacrificed.

The simplest case is illustrated in Figure 9.2. The indifference curves (I_0, I_1, I_2, etc.) represent combinations of disposable income and leisure between which the individual is indifferent. Higher indifference curves reflect higher levels of welfare. The budget line indicates that a maximum of L hours of leisure can be taken per period (i.e., 168 per week). If all these hours were instead worked, then disposable income would be Y (i.e., the hourly wage rate net of tax multiplied by 168 hours). Thus, the slope of the budget line, YL, is the net wage rate, $w(1-t_0)$, where w is the gross wage rate and t_0 is the tax rate. To maximise welfare, the individual will therefore choose the combination of disposable income and leisure at which the highest attainable indifference curve (in this case, I_1) is just tangential to the budget line, YL. In Figure 9.2, this is at point A, which is associated with a disposable income, Y_0, and work hours, $L-L_0$ (NB: hours of work are measured to the left from L, where L is equal to zero hours worked).

Any change in the tax rate, t, will alter the slope of the budget line, YL. Suppose, for example, that the government reduces the rate of tax from t_0 to t_1 (see Figure 9.3). The budget line would become steeper, since by working all the hours available, the individual can now earn a higher disposable income, Y', rather than Y. In other words, the new budget line, $Y'L$, now has a greater slope, $w(1-t_1)$. Equilibrium will now be achieved at point B, which is on a higher indifference curve (I_3) than before, indicating an increase in the individual's welfare. But while a tax reduction un-ambiguously increases welfare, does it lead to an increase in the number of hours worked?

In fact, there are two effects involved. The first is the 'substitution effect'. Because the tax reduction has altered the relative 'price' of leisure *vis-à-vis* work, increasing the opportunity cost of leisure in terms of income forgone, the individual will tend to substitute work for leisure. The second is the income effect. Because a given number of hours work now

FIGURE 9.2
The Income/Leisure Trade-off

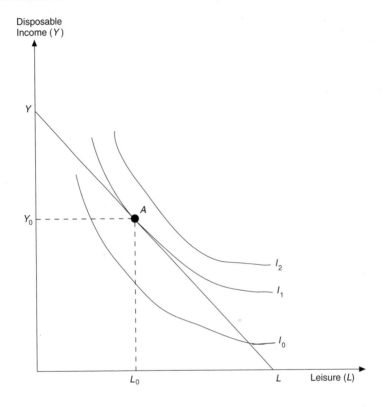

yields a higher disposable income, the individual can effectively have more of both income and leisure than before, by working fewer hours (at a higher, post-tax rate) for a higher income.

The impact of the two effects on hours worked can be disentangled in Figure 9.3 in the following way, remembering at the same time that although leisure is measured along the horizontal axis, $L-L_0$ is the amount of work the individual would undertake if the individual were at A. The diagram indicates that the individual would start at A and after the tax reduction would end up at B, on a higher indifference curve. Suppose we take the individual at point B and remove just enough income to force this individual back to the original indifference curve, I_1. Removing income

FIGURE 9.3
Reduction in Taxes and the Income/Leisure Choice

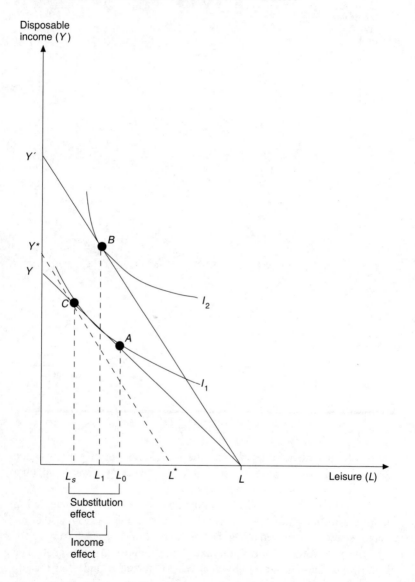

does not alter the slope of the constraint line but causes a parallel shift to the left. Such a constraint line is shown as Y^*L^*. As the diagram indicates, the individual would now not choose to be at A since C is just tangential to the original indifference curve with a constraint line Y^*L^*. Here L–L_s hours would be worked. The difference between the number of hours worked before, L–L_0, and the number worked due to the tax reduction ignoring the income effect, L–L_s, is L_0–L_s. This is a measure of the substitution effect. Following the tax cut, the substitution effect is away from leisure and towards work.

The rest of the change in the number of hours worked must be due to the income effect. That is the movement from C to B when we restore the income back to the individual. In this case, while the substitution effect alone would have increased the number of hours worked from L–L_0 to L–L_s, the overall increase is only from L–L_0 to L–L_1. In other words, the income effect reduces the number of hours worked by L_1–L_s. In general, therefore, following a reduction in the rate of tax, basic economic theory suggests that there will be a positive substitution effect towards hours worked, causing people to work more hours, and a negative income effect, encouraging people to work fewer hours. Conversely we could say that there is a negative substitution effect away from leisure and a positive income effect to take on more leisure. Notice that there is nothing inherent in the theory reviewed above to suggest that the (positive) substitution effect towards hours worked will always outweigh the (negative) income effect away from work. It is theoretically possible that, far from strengthening the supply side in the sense of increasing the incentive to work, tax cuts may actually reduce the supply of labour. Figure 9.4 shows how, with different relative preferences between disposable income and leisure (i.e., differently shaped indifference curves), the same reduction in the tax rate can lead to a reduction in the number of hours worked, from L–L_0 to L–L_1.

Social security benefits can be introduced into this analysis fairly simply (see Figure 9.5). Social security normally provides unemployed individuals with a basic income, here LB_0, for which they do not have to work. However, once they begin working, benefits are typically withdrawn as disposable income rises, until at some point ,Y_b, disposable income is deemed sufficiently high that no benefits are payable. Figure 9.5 illustrates a situation in which benefits are withdrawn slowly enough so that each extra hour worked always increases disposable income. Significantly, in the British social security system, there are actually points along the budget constraint at which an extra hour worked reduces disposable income. Because the sudden withdrawal of a benefit – e.g., free school meals – occurs at a discrete level of income, it means that if this trigger level of income is only marginally exceeded, a £1 increase in gross income may make a family worse off.

FIGURE 9.4
Alternative Income/Leisure Choice Decision after the Result of a Tax Change

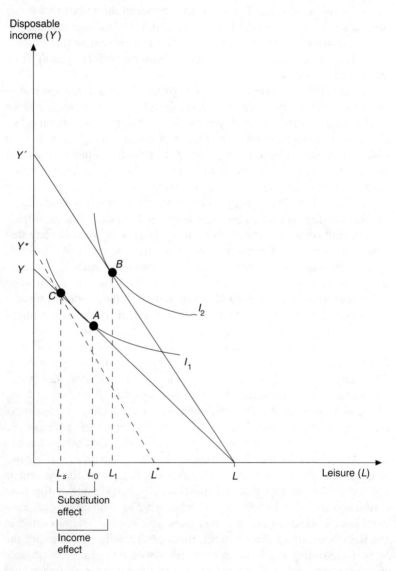

FIGURE 9.5
Impact of Social Security Benefits on Income/Leisure Choices

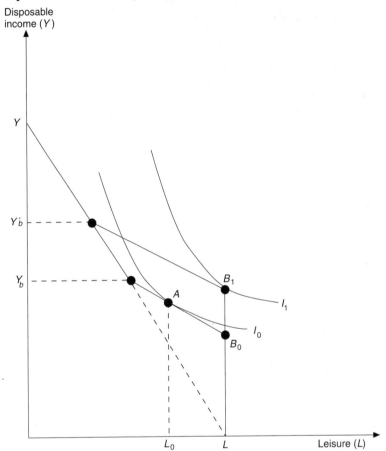

Even in the less extreme case shown in Figure 9.5, it can be seen that a rise in social security benefits paid to the unemployed (from LB_0 to LB_1) may result in an individual who was previously welfare-maximising at a point A (i.e., working $L-L_0$ hours) and receiving earned income and benefits, choosing instead to withdraw his or her labour altogether. The new welfare-maximising equilibrium is at point B_1 on indifference curve, I_1, at which the individual is (quite rationally) choosing to be unemployed (i.e., to work zero hours) since B_1 lies on a higher indifference curve. It follows that a reduction in unemployment-related benefits will tend to increase the number of hours offered for work.

Basic economic theory therefore suggests that, provided that the substitution effect outweighs the income effect, tax cuts will tend to increase the incentive to work, while reductions in unemployment-related benefits will have a similarly beneficial effect on the labour supply. Against this background, tax and social security policy since 1979 has been designed to increase the supply of labour (see also Chapter 7). Between 1979 and 1992, the marginal rate of income tax paid by top income earners was cut from 83 per cent (98 per cent for unearned income from investments) to 40 per cent, one of the lowest top rates in the European Community. The basic rate was similarly cut from an inherited rate of 33 per cent to 25 per cent though subsequently the first £2000 was to be taxed at 20 per cent. All other marginal income tax rates were abolished.

Social security has also been overhauled in an attempt to increase the supply of labour and end the so-called 'unemployment trap'. This term refers to the situation in which an individual who finds, due to the payment of taxes on earned income and the withdrawal of benefits, that he or she has almost as high a disposable income when unemployed as if he or she worked; in other words, there is no financial incentive to seek work. The extent of this disincentive is captured by the so-called 'replacement ratio' (R), which is defined as the ratio of total benefits while unemployed (B) to disposable income while in work (Y_d):

$$R = \frac{B}{Y_d}$$

For an unskilled worker with dependent partner and school-aged children, total unemployment-related benefits may be high relative to the disposable income that could be expected from work, resulting in a replacement ratio which may be close to, or even above, unity. The Government has therefore sought in its reforms to reduce replacement ratios, in attempt to discourage 'voluntary' unemployment.

Training and Education: the Key to Higher Productivity

The primary role of training and education is to increase the quality of the workforce, the vast majority of whom are in continuous employment. And it is the British system of training and education which has long been regarded as the root cause of the economy's poor productivity record.

TABLE 9.4
International Comparisons of Human Capital Acquisition

	Britain	France	Germany	Japan	United States
Average Years in Formal Education	11.3	11.6	9.6	11.7	13.4
16–24 year olds in further education (%)	36	n/a	45	54	73
School-leavers Entering Higher Education (%)	14	35	30	n/a	54
Engineering Graduates per '000 of Population	14	15	21	35	n/a
Top Managers with Degrees (%)	24	65	62	85	85

SOURCE   Haskel, A. and Kay, J. (1990) 'Productivity in British Industry', in Cogden, T. *et al.*, *The State* of *the Economy*, IEA, London.

Table 9.4 illustrates that on almost all measures of human capital acquisition, Britain compares unfavourably with the other major economies. Britain has a relatively low proportion of 16–24 year olds in further education and the least-educated managerial class in Europe. While the Conservative Government has laid great emphasis recently on widening access to higher education in Britain, forecasting that by the year 2000 one in three 18-year-olds will enter university or college, it appears to be in the area of further education and skills training (particularly on-the-job training and day-release training for blue-collar workers) that Britain most lags behind its international competitors. The greatest decline has been in the number of apprentices undergoing training (see Table 9.5).

The low level of training by companies is believed to stem from the nature of the British labour market, in which workers expect to move jobs frequently – in contrast to Japan, for example, where workers often stay with the same employer throughout their working lives. This mobility reduces the incentive for firms to train their staff. Rather than expensively training workers who may then move to rival firms, it is more cost-effective for each firm to 'free-ride', waiting for others to pay for training

TABLE 9.5
Apprentices in British Manufacturing Industries

Year	Number of Apprentices	Percentage of Workforce
1964	240,400	3.0
1974	139,600	2.0
1979	155,000	2.2
1984	82,000	1.5
1989	53,600	1.0

SOURCE   *Employment Gazette*, table 1.14, various issues, HMSO, London.

and then 'poaching' trained staff by paying marginally higher wages. The result is that, at an economy-wide level, there is a tendency for British firms collectively to undertrain staff, damaging their longer-term competitiveness. Table 9.6 highlights that, during the boom of the late 1980s, the percentage of firms reporting that their expansion was constrained by their inability to recruit skilled staff was many times above Continental levels.

TABLE 9.6
Firms Constrained by Skill Shortages (%)

Year	Britain	France	Germany	Italy
1987	21.0	2.8	2.8	1.0
1988	26.3	3.8	3.0	2.0
1989	19.3	5.3	6.8	2.8

SOURCES   European Commission (1991) and *ad hoc* labour market surveys, 1985–1989 in *The European Economy*, Brussels, 1991.

The problem of market failure in the area of skills training appears to be, paradoxically, exacerbated by the Government's efforts to reduce the power of trade unions and thereby improve the flexibility of the labour market. Trade union reforms, taken together with other employment measures to make it easier to hire and fire workers, have had the effect of significantly strengthening the 'external labour market'; that is, making it easier for firms to release unwanted labour into, and draw needed workers out of, the pool of unemployed labour. In other words, it is now much less costly than hitherto for firms to adjust their employment in line with production, by hiring and firing employees. In the past, in contrast, getting rid of unwanted staff was difficult and costly, so that many firms were chronically overmanned for extended periods and others preferred to (inefficiently) use their existing workforces more intensively in boom periods (e.g., by working them longer hours and paying overtime), in preference to taking on additional workers who might subsequently prove hard to sack.

But the side-effect of a stronger external labour market is a natural tendency for firms to look outside for skilled labour whenever their requirements change. For example, when the advent of computerised typesetting altered the nature of newspaper typesetting jobs, several national dailies simply fired their existing printworkers and hired electrical workers who already possessed the appropriate skills. In contrast, consider the position in Germany, where stringent labour laws make firing workers very difficult, and Japan, where many workers enjoy jobs for life with the same company. In both these countries, the external labour market is weak. The idea of systematically hiring and firing labour in line with planned output is relatively alien. One consequence is that overmanning during recessions is commonplace. The positive dimension, however, is that when the nature of the demand for labour changes (e.g., due the introduction of a new production process), the onus is on German and Japanese firms to retrain the existing labour forces, rather than simply bidding for previously trained workers in the external labour market. Moreover, not only does the existence of a weak external labour market force such firms to look inwards and train, but they can also be confident (unlike their British rivals) that expenditure on training will not simply lead to trained staff being poached by free-riders. Thus, one unintended consequence of the Government's labour union reforms may have been actually to exacerbate the market failure that causes Britain to under-invest in skills training – with all that implies for the longer-term rate of economic growth.

Quality and Flexibility in the Labour Market

It is not only the quantity but also the quality of labour that can be related to the growth process. Moreover, we could argue that flexibility is almost equally important. This chapter has highlighted the possibility that trades unions may inhibit growth by resisting the introduction of new processes and working practices and has reviewed the measures that the Conservative Government has taken since 1979 to alter the balance of power in the labour market. Other obstacles to the flexible operation of the labour market, which may inhibit growth, have also been identified, notably excessive taxes on labour and inappropriately designed systems of unemployment benefit, which raise replacement ratios unduly high. The Government's attempts to reform the tax and social security systems in an effort to increase incentives to work have also been briefly discussed. Provided the substitution effect outweighs the income effect, tax cuts will increase the incentive to work. On a similar theme, if benefits are reduced or not index-linked then there is, too, an additional 'incentive' to return to work. But even if employment can be found, what kind of jobs exist? Britain has a relatively poor record on investment in human capital, particularly by the private sector in the area of skills training. The continuing relatively low level of human capital accumulation in Britain suggests the worrying possibility that recent measures to strengthen the external labour market through legislative reform may actually have exacerbated the market failures that appear to inhibit private-sector investment in worker training.

The Role of the European Union

10

Even before Britain's membership of the Community, its trade with the European Union (EU) was becoming increasingly important and was growing faster than its trade with the Commonwealth. Prior to its entry, the UK government placed great emphasis on the dynamic effects of EU membership. Producers, governments argued, would have a much larger 'home' market and thus firms would benefit from economies of scale. The increased competition from abroad would force UK firms to become more efficient, would lead them to invest more, improve their expenditure on R&D and thereby aid the growth process. So what went wrong? One estimate was that as a result of joining the EU, UK imports of manufactures increased by £8 billion from her new partners, home sales fell by £4.5 billion and exports to non-partners fell by £1.5 billion. Britain's trade balance was worsened and output of manufactures fell by at least 1.5 per cent of GDP. A problem for UK industry was structural rigidity which prevented better economic performance, certainly in the short term. Moreover, the role of state procurement in all EU countries prevented competition and gave little incentive for efficiency. These barriers in existence during the first two decades of UK membership are still in evidence despite efforts to dismantle them and are a major hurdle for firms such as those in the UK whose markets have been subject to reduced government support.

State Aids to Industry

One of the basic principles on which the European Union was built was that of the creation and maintenance of a system of free and undistorted competition. Subsidies risk threatening the efficient functioning of this system as they tend to reduce efficiency and distort trade in a manner similar to that of protectionist measures. The benefits from the Single European Market (SEM) will only materialise if governments do not bias the adjustment process through the use of state aids. Within the EU these state aids or subsidies are used, for example, to encourage the use of public transportation, the intensification of R&D, and the support of declining industries. Not only do the subsidies distort the market but the taxes raised to provide the subsidies add a further problem in reducing international welfare. Moreover, in the effort to obtain subsidies and to retaliate against others who have them uses up resources and further incurs a welfare loss.

The level of these subsidies in the EU is difficult to establish. A survey undertaken by the Commission in 1990 revealed that there were on average around ECU82 billion of state aids in the Member States between 1986 and 1988, amounting to 2.2 per cent of Community GDP and 4.5 per cent of total general government expenditure in the Community. There were also major differences by state, with the UK and Belgium spending approximately 1 per cent of GDP on state aids, whilst Italy, the Netherlands and France spent 3 per cent or more, as Table 10.1 indicates.

Furthermore, the subsidies are industry-specific, around 60 per cent went on three sectors, transport (30%), the coal industry (16%) and agri-

TABLE 10.1
Subsidies as a Percentage of GDP

Country	1960	1975–9	1985–9
Austria	0.5	3.0	3.0
Belgium	1.3	1.4	1.3
Denmark	0.7	3.1	3.1
France	1.6	2.5	3.0
Germany	0.8	2.1	2.2
Italy	1.4	3.2	3.3
Japan	0.4	1.3	1.1
Netherlands	1.2	2.4	3.7
Sweden	1.0	3.9	4.7
UK	1.9	2.7	1.7

SOURCE   Adapted from Crafts, N. (1992), 'Productivity Growth Reconsidered', *Economic Policy*, vol. 15, October, p. 411.

culture/fisheries (13%). The remaining 40 per cent went mainly to manufacturing, with the main sectors being cars, electronics and aviation. The subsidisation of these sectors is particularly high in Greece, Spain, France and Portugal. Concerning horizontal aids which have no sectoral or regional specificity, there is heavy subsidisation of trade/export in Greece, Ireland, France, Belgium; of general investment in Portugal, Belgium, the Netherlands, Luxembourg; and of small and medium-sized enterprises in the Netherlands, Belgium, Greece, Italy and Luxembourg. Whilst these are in existence UK manufacturing cannot be said to face a level playing field in its competition in Europe. In addition they may not only make UK exports less price-competitive, but reduce the price of imports into the UK. These state aids can also be used to lower the cost of capital and can be used for the education of the workforce, both factors which we have seen are important in the growth process. If we do not tackle the issues of state aids then inefficient firms will remain in the market and poor productivity performance will be encouraged not only in the UK but also in France and Germany.

Mergers

Connected to this area of state aids is the role of merger and acquisition behaviour in the Community. The SEM which was supposed to lead to greater competition between companies has triggered off a merger boom in Europe. Aside from the question as to which countries are the major players in the takeover market, mergers may impose costs on society. In order to protect the public, countries usually resort to antitrust or monopolies and mergers legislation. The problem in the Community is that not all countries possess such policies and those that do differ in the extent to which their policies operate. At the one end of the continuum we have the UK and Germany which have well developed rules, whilst at the other we have Denmark, Greece and Italy which have very flexible regimes.

In this merger boom there is the potential to abuse market power. Within the European framework the pressure is on those countries which do not currently possess a well-developed merger and acquisitions policy to establish one which is as lenient as possible, thereby encouraging their own national 'champions'. This will give their own firms an advantage in the market and the possibility is there for them to drive out from the market other firms which are subject to more strict rules on size. In addition, although it was UK firms in Europe who were first off the mark in the current European merger boom, French firms have become very active in the market during the early 1990s. There is resentment from some quarters that these firms, aided by the fact that a number of them have sizeable government shareholdings, are receiving government aid via loans and lower interest rates. This allows them to be very active in the merger process, in a way that damages fair competition.

Regional Policy

State aids are permitted in the EU where there are regional problems, important projects of Community interest or the development of certain economic activities. In particular, Community state aid policy is to assure that national state aids are compatible with the improvement of regional cohesion. Aid in this area includes money from the European Regional Development Fund (ERDF), European Social Fund (ESF), European Agricultural Guidance and Guarantee Fund (EAGGF) and European Investment Bank (EIB).

Regional problems for the UK are the same as those for the Community. Peripheral areas tend to be less industrialised and have a greater reliance on agriculture. They may have structural weaknesses, being historically reliant on now declining industries, and tend to exhibit higher than average levels of unemployment. Neo-classical theory suggests that with perfect mobility of the factors of production, such as labour and capital, poorer regions with cheaper labour will attract investment. In practice, however, factors of production are not very mobile and historically capital tends to be drawn towards the most prosperous areas since they offer higher rates of return. Moreover, larger companies have favoured proximity to highly industrialised or urban centres since this gives them access to capital markets and to external economies of scale.

If this is the picture in the UK, then a similar one could be painted for Europe. The impact of the SEM may well exacerbate the regional disparities between the individual countries in the Community. Industries in the Golden Triangle of London–Hamburg–Turin benefit the most and peripheral regions such as the rest of the UK, Portugal, Spain and Greece are the main losers. Although regional policy has attempted to mollify these regional differences it has on the whole been inadequate to deal with the problems. For example, regional policy in the Community accounted for only 8 per cent of the Community's budget in 1990, far less than the 62 per cent spent on supporting agriculture and only around 1 per cent of the EC countries' GDP. This means that unless the appropriate measures are taken at national and Community levels the regional problems will worsen during the 1990s. The disparity between richer and poorer nations and regions will widen, and convergence between countries is unlikely to occur.

Larger companies are likely to draw the greatest advantage from the SEM whilst medium-sized firms in low-productivity areas, which to some extent depend upon frictions and impediments in the market, will find acute problems of competition in the enlarged market. There is also the possibility that firms and resources will relocate to exploit the comparative advantage of different regions. There is evidence of this actually occurring with US firms looking more towards central Europe for growth and acquisition rather than their traditional location of the UK. Consequently, the integration process may have adverse sectorial and regional effects on the problems in the Community and those in the UK in particular.

Social Policies

Social and regional inequalities often overlap, but there are also separate and persistent social differences both at Community and country level. Social policy at a national level includes issues such as social security payments, unemployment benefits, health, education and housing, but EU social policy is much more narrowly defined, concentrating primarily on labour market issues. These include pay equalities for women, education and training, labour mobility and employees' rights. The latter were consolidated in the development of the Social Charter. This was an attempt to safeguard the rights of employees whilst at the same time setting out the major tenets on which the pattern of labour law and, more generally, the European concept of society and the place of labour in that society should be based. The Charter, which is a nonbinding declaration of principles, will be followed by a work programme of action for its implementation. As we now know, this was not adopted by the UK. One important reason for not adopting the Charter in the UK was the perceived problem of union representation on boards of directors, but perhaps the UK believed that there was a further advantage from the non-adoption of the Charter. Avoiding minimum-wage legislation would help UK industry, which has tended to have lower productivity levels even after the catchup spurt of the 1980s. This would lead to more inward investment and so reduce the balance of payments constraint, leading to higher long-term growth. It waits to be seen whether more extensive social policies are a natural complement to the internal market, or significantly detract from it by confronting businesses with higher labour costs. In particular we should be concerned about small to medium-sized enterprises whose proportion of labour costs are higher than the large multinational corporations.

Because the UK lies on the periphery of the Community the establishment of the SEM is likely to exacerbate its problems. Without sufficient regional and social funding, resources will migrate towards the South-East, the UK's most congested region. This will be enhanced by the development of the Channel tunnel. For the UK both the limited regional funds available and their insufficient concentration on its problems have reduced the effectiveness of EU policy. UK regions now receive even less as a result of the southern enlargement of Spain, Portugal and Greece. UK rural areas, which are above the EU's new GDP per capita guidelines, seem likely to suffer. This will eventually be followed by the UK'S depressed industrial areas. Given the fact that UK regional funding has actually reduced by half during the 1980s, the UK regions have had to tap EU funds even more. But even here the funding has not always had an industrial bias for over 60 per cent of funding for the regions in the period 1973–86 had a predominantly agricultural flavour. The UK did receive in January 1994 the largest share in the Community of structural funding (30.4%) for industrial and urban areas in decline, but the amount of ECU 2.142 million was fairly small in relation to the overall EU budget and the 1990s may well see a further widening of regional disparities both in the UK and within Europe. Thus we can perhaps see why, as with peripheral regions in general, the UK has sought to remain competitive through being a low-wage economy. The risk is that, given greater freedom of locational choice in the new more integrated Europe, we may end up with a two-tier Europe. In the first tier we will see those areas where there are large, well-developed local labour markets in relatively high-skilled, highly educated or highly paid jobs. These areas will become the focus for relatively high-productivity, high-skill and probably high-cost activities. In the lower tier will be areas that compete for the more routine activities in both manufacturing and service industries, where costs are low and the opportunities for skill development are limited.

Increased Competition from the Newly Industrialised Countries

We have concentrated on growth in the developed countries in this book, and in the UK in particular. Growth has tended to fluctuate over time in these countries though on the whole has tended to be positive. Other countries have not been so fortunate, with many parts of Africa and Latin America experiencing positive growth often outweighed by periods of negative growth. There are some countries whose growth performance over the last 30 years has been relatively spectacular and these have been termed the newly industrialised countries (NICs). In this group we would include South Korea, Taiwan, Hong Kong, Singapore, Thailand, Malaysia, Indonesia, Mainland China, Argentina, Brazil and Mexico. By the mid1980s seven of them were amongst the world's 20 largest exporters. All these countries are 'outward looking', export activity being the basis for their high levels of growth, although there are other factors to consider since growth is associated with large rates of capital accumulation, both human and nonhuman. In 1991, for example, Taiwan accounted for around a quarter of the doctorates in engineering in American universities.

Whereas some of these countries were satisfied with low-level technology products at the start of their growth cycle, capital accumulation by raising wage rates has caused these countries to shift away from more labour-intensive production processes. Thus, for example, Japan has moved out of shipbuilding to be replaced by South Korea. The process, therefore, is that by capital accumulation these NICs have become a threat to many developed economies especially in the areas of trade in intermediate products, natural resources and producer goods. Thus many of these economies exhibit rapid technological progress resulting in the quality upgrading of exports. Sometimes this process has been encouraged by the imposition of voluntary export restraints (VERs) imposed by developed economies on the NICs which have responded by upgrading the quality of their exports. It follows, therefore, that a developed economy which does not move on to higher technology products but stays with lower value-added, labour-intensive products, through choice or because it has not invested enough in capital equipment or human capital, will face increasing pressure in many of its traditional export and domestic markets. In fact this process is not new, it has been long recognised that the lower an industry's value-added per worker the more likely are developing countries and NICs to be its exporters. In other words, developing countries have to continue moving upwards in the production of higher and higher valued-added products. For the UK the problem of concentrating on low-wage, low-technology and low value-added products is clear.

As an example of products in which the EU in general and the UK in particular have been losing ground, we could look to the steel industry or the clothing and textile industry. In the case of the latter the intense competition from low-cost producers saw the share of imports in EU consumption rise from 18 per cent in 1975 to 45 per cent in 1985. We can see the problems faced by the EU and the UK if we look at the geographical spread of extra-Community exports. Both for Japan and the NICs imports into the EU exceed exports from the EU. For less developed countries (LDCs) the reverse is true. Thus by directing a steadily increasing proportion of their exports to non-industrialised countries, the EU are

TABLE 10.2
World FDI Outward Investment Flows (%)

Country	1982	1989
US	49.2	20
EC	30.5	45
NICs	5.0	10
Others	15.3	25

SOURCE   Cook, M. and Healey, N.M. (1990), *Topics in International Economics*, Anforme; Griffiths, A. and Wall, S. (1993) *Applied Economics*, 5th edn, Longman.

managing to continue to export but their products embody lower levels of technology. If this is the case for the EU, then the same, if not more, will be true for the UK. Thus because the UK's exports to countries like the US, Japan and the NICs are less than our imports from them, the UK has come to rely on a small group of markets, such as LDC or OPEC countries. Unfortunately, the fluctuations in sales and the risks of trading in these markets are high, leading to uncertainty in export orders and the problems of not being able to plan on a long-term basis. As an indication of the growing presence from the NICs we only need to consider Table 10.2. In only five years their outward investment flows have doubled, giving an indication of their growing confidence in external markets in general and exports in particular. Even with the growth of non-tariff barriers to trade, import ratios for NIC manufacturing imports rose more than threefold in most of the major EU countries.

Multinationals and Foreign Direct Investment

Behind the structural changes in many economies have been changes in the competitive structure of markets through the growth of firms, especially multinational enterprises (MNEs). A multinational enterprise or company can be defined as an organisation which owns and controls production or service facilities outside the country in which it is based. Table 10.3 shows the top 20 multinational companies and indicates their diversity of country or origin and that their sales can exceed the GDP of many small developing countries. What Table 10.3 does not tell us, however, is how MNEs have grown over time, with the Americans dominating the scene in the early 1950s and 1960s, to be challenged by the European

TABLE 10.3
Largest Non-financial Multinationals, 1990, Ranked by Foreign Assets ($)

Rank		Industry	Country	Foreign Assets	Total Assets
1.	Royal Dutch/Shell	Oil	UK/Holland	n/a	106.3
2.	Ford Motor	Cars/Trucks	US	55.2	173.7
3.	General Motors	Cars/Trucks	US	52.6	180.2
4.	Exxon	Oil	US	51.6	87.7
5.	IBM	Computers	US	45.7	87.6
6.	BP	Oil	UK	39.7	59.3
7.	Nestle	Food	Switzerland	n/a	27.9
8.	Unilever	Food	UK/Holland	n/a	24.8
9.	Asea Brown Boveri	Electrical	Swiss/Sweden	n/a	30.2
10.	Philips	Electronics	Holland	n/a	30.6
11.	Alcatel Alsthom	Telecoms	France	n/a	38.2
12.	Mobil	Oil	US	22.3	41.7
13.	Fiat	Cars/Trucks	Italy	19.5	66.3
14.	Siemens	Electrical	Germany	n/a	50.1
15.	Hanson	Diversified	UK	n/a	27.7
16.	Volkswagen	Cars/Trucks	Germany	n/a	41.9
17.	Elf Aquitaine	Oil	France	17.0	42.6
18.	Mitsubishi	Trading	Japan	16.7	73.8
19.	General Electric	Diversified	US	16.5	153.9
20.	Mitsui	Trading	Japan	5.0	60.8

SOURCE *The Economist*, 27 March 1993.

MNEs, Japanese MNEs and the growing threat of MNEs from the NICs during the 1980 and 1990s. In fact, in 1970 of the 7000 MNEs identified by the UN more than half were from the US and the UK. In the 1990s just under half of the world's 35,000 MNEs were from America, Japan, Germany and Switzerland, with the UK lying in seventh place. This growth in cross-border activity has been driven forward by a number of factors: falling regulatory barriers to overseas investment, reductions in telecommunications and transportation costs and the relaxation of constraints on domestic and international capital markets. So how has the UK fared in this growth of MNE activity and what has been its impact on the UK economy?

With regard to foreign direct investment (FDI), the UK has historically been a net creditor as Table 10.4 indicates, though as we can see by the early 1990s there was more FDI arriving in the UK than leaving it. The US heads the list of sources, with the EU now contributing almost 30 per cent, and there is a growing importance in FDI from Japan. There has been a decline in FDI activity in the manufacturing sector in the UK, compensated by a large upsurge in activity of FDI in insurance, banking and property. In terms of net manufacturing FDI the UK has tended to invest abroad in less technology-intensive industries whereas it is host to com-

TABLE 10.4
Net Foreign Investment Flows for the UK (£ Million)

Year	Outward	Inward
1980	3,391	2,541
1981	4,671	980
1982	2,122	1,137
1983	3,460	2,063
1984	5,929	−246
1985	8,836	4,123
1986	11,641	4,078
1987	19,041	8,508
1988	20,758	8,990
1989	19,164	15,848
1990	9,600	18,593
1991	10,810	11,958

SOURCES   *British Business*, 17 May 1985, 11 March 1988, London; *Business Briefing*, 1992, British Chambers of Commerce, Chester.

panies which are more technology-intensive. If these foreign companies have higher levels of productivity than UK companies, then on an aggregate basis UK productivity levels will rise. Conversely UK competitors in these markets may well find that if they cannot adapt quickly enough they will be forced to leave the market. The reasons why the UK has suffered from a declining share in manufacturing FDI are various. Most of these are location-specific, such as higher relative inflation in the UK, lack of a long-term industrial policy, and the better growth prospects of other European countries. None the less, it has been pointed out that the scenario has changed quite dramatically during the 1980s and 1990s. The UK has become a relatively strike-free area, has one of the lowest rates of corporation and income taxes compared with its major competitors in Europe, has a very efficient transportation and communication system and also benefits from a transparent system of public administration. However, it could be that there are market-based forces which drive FDI activity. Companies who understand the needs of their customers will do well when faced with competition from domestic firms. Because UK companies may well have lagged behind in understanding their customers' needs, foreign companies which were further along that route displaced indigenous firms in the market. Conversely, this lack of understanding customer needs may also be an explanation of why UK companies have not faired well in high-technology markets abroad. Given the ebb and flow of overall FDI and MNE activity, what has been the impact on the UK economy?

Employment and Trade Effects

The employment effects of MNEs depend upon the degree to which foreign MNEs reduce their workforces more in times of recession than do domestic companies, that foreign MNEs are more capital-intensive and therefore replace labour on a gradual basis, the degree to which domestic companies cannot compete with the foreign MNE and the 'rationalisation' decisions of UK MNEs to locate production outside the UK.

Evidence seems to suggest that during periods of economic stability MNEs add to employment opportunities. During recessionary periods, however, they offer no more of a safe haven than do domestic companies. Since MNEs are constantly reappraising their location decisions there are many instances, such as Dunlop and ICI, where companies have reduced employment in the UK whilst at the same time expanding employment elsewhere. Such a situation is occurring now within the whole of the EU where MNEs are relocating some of their activities to cheaper wage sites in Eastern Europe. A *Financial Times* survey in 1993 noted that for engineers the UK is the cheapest source in Western Europe but Czech costs are almost 50 per cent less ('UK Relocation', *The Financial Times*, 28 May 1993).

Foreign participation in an industry also appears to have important export and trade implications. The greater the level of foreign participation in an industry, the relatively more favourable is the balance of trade. In other words, foreign-owned firms are responsible for a larger share of the host countries' exports and imports than they are in sales and investment. As an example of this we could point to the deficit on the trade account in colour televisions, which became a surplus of £446 million in 1991.

Technology Transfer

On one level the impact of FDI and MNE activity on the UK economy in terms of technology is for foreign companies to bring higher and better levels of technology, and their associated working practices, to the UK market, which increases both production and productivity. These technological leads and lags can be important determinants of differences amongst the OECD countries in growth and trade performance. One factor that seems to be important is that technologies are not readily and easily available to, or assimilated by, all firms and countries. In this case, once a country falls behind in a certain level of technology then it will have difficulty catching up. Technological development is cumulative in nature, derives from learning by doing and is costly to assimilate. Existing firms continue to move onwards and upwards to protect their positions in the market. One factor that may be important here is the level of private-sector-funded civilian R&D: countries such as Sweden and Japan top the list of those allocating most civilian resources to R&D and both appear to be successful in assimilating others' ideas as well as developing their own. This notion could also explain why countries like the UK which devote a smaller proportion of resources to private R&D have fallen behind in a number of fields and the role of governments in stimulating R&D may crowd out private-sector R&D. Moreover, given scarce high-skilled human resources, once these are lost to a competitor, there may be little alternative for competing companies than to move to other markets, often producing lower level technology products.

We have seen how the UK has tended to be the location for high-technology FDI. If this leads to sectors dominated by foreign companies then the barriers to entry may be sufficiently large to prevent entry of indigenous firms. In other words, the technology transfer has little impact on domestic companies. What of R&D? Given the growth in FDI does this mean that there is a corresponding growth in R&D in the recipient country which will benefit the economy generally through the trickle-down effect? There is evidence to suggest that foreign companies are more willing to locate their R&D in the host economy, though the variations between sectors are substantial. Moreover, the type of R&D may be MNE-specific rather than for more general consumption.

Given the arguments specified above we would expect that if the UK has suffered from its inability to provide high-technology exports, then the inflow of foreign FDI and MNEs in the high-technology area should help to rectify this problem. However, there is an argument that the reason why foreign MNEs wish to enter the UK market is to exploit their ownership-specific advantages; that is, to gain market share in the UK rather than as a means for the UK to export high-technology products. In addition, the skill and R&D intensity of UK imports of goods and FDI appears to have increased over time, widening the gap between UK exports and outward FDI flows. Thus if the markets into which the UK is selling her products are made up of more mature, lower-technology products and also markets in which the number of competitors are growing, especially from the emerging NICs, then this does not auger well for the UK's trading performance. Moreover, if the demand for high-technology products is more inelastic than low-technology products and the rate of growth of the former markets is greater, then the UK will face further problems in trying to recover its position in the overall world trade league. Thus since the UK does not seem to benefit greatly from high-technology inflows this merely reinforces the technological gap that already exists between the UK and the rest of the world and reduces the ability of the UK economy to compete successfully on world markets.

It is important to examine the role of the state in 'correcting' market failure with regard to R&D and technology. Government support of strategic industries, their national champions, appears not to have been a success in the UK. Subsidising these companies or enabling them to have a degree of protection has resulted in them being more inefficient than their major competitors. Moreover, supporting showpiece projects even beyond the point where they are viable has actually led to funds being switched to support these companies during recessionary periods, starving new technological industries of finance and resources.

Once an economy has fallen behind, technology is not something that can be taken off the shelf and superimposed from one economy to another. It takes time to gather the skills, equipment and organisation, and to embody these in people and institutions. Because we require all these pieces to be in place, it might explain the uneven pattern of development between countries and industries notwithstanding the presence of MNEs which might be expected to smooth out these differences. This diffusion of ideas follows an S-shaped path through the economy: the innovation is taken up slowly at first, then by a rapidly increasing number of companies, followed by the stragglers. Because technological advance is more often embodied in new investment, technological advance happens more quickly in industries that are expanding rapidly rather than the mature industrial sectors in which many of the UK's manufacturing firms find themselves.

As support for this notion we can look to the difficulty UK manufacturing has in managing innovation. They are less likely to undertake strategic alignments and there is an absence of an industry-based mechanism to allow firms to collaborate. They can buy in technology, but the lack of long-term vision leads firms to rely on short-term market research. When changes in the market occur, other firms which have been undertaking long-term research are better placed.

The UK's Educated Labour Force

One of the factors that has been highlighted in the above discussion of R&D, innovation and MNEs is the need for a highly trained workforce. Although some of the supply-side solutions to this problem have been discussed in Chapters 5 and 6, badly or inappropriately trained workforces and managers may be unable to cope with the changes that are being foisted on them. The lower emphasis on training by British industry has been outlined in Chapter 9, and although skill shortages in the UK have diminished, primarily due to the rise in unemployment during the current recession, skill deficiencies are likely to re-emerge in the future. In particular, the Department of Employment has pointed to the need by firms to develop skills and training in white-collar workers in the areas of managerial, professional and associated professional/technical occupations. In addition 60 per cent of firms were concerned that their average skill needs from employees were increasing. The effective application of new technologies will require not only specific technical skills, for which in the area of National Vocational Qualification (NVQ) levels 3 and 4 Britain still lags far behind France and Germany, but also managers will need a better awareness of the scope to use technology to improve products and processes, and implement the organisational changes that may be needed to get the full benefits from improved technology. Increasing emphasis on quality and innovation will demand more skills throughout the workforce and again may be the catalyst for organisational change. There is a need to bring the idea of innovation and the diffusion of these notions into the educational training forum. A workforce which is highly trained at the top end in the development of ideas and innovation may be ineffectual in the processes used by industry and its take-up of ideas if the workforce lower down is ill-educated.

The Exhaustion of North Sea Oil

Both in Chapter 1 and in Chapter 2 we outlined the impact of North Sea oil on the balance of payments. This has shown up in these accounts in four ways. First, there is the balance of trade in oil and gas; secondly, there is the net purchase of goods and services required to discover and extract the oil and gas; thirdly, there are the capital inflows to finance the discovery and extraction stages; and finally, there is the requirement to pay interest, profits and dividends at a later date on these earlier capital inflows. The oil balance has clearly worsened since 1986 (see Table 4.1), though it still stays in surplus. In other words, the net revenue from North Sea oil is unlikely to offset any further deterioration in the deficit on manufactures. Though we cannot be sure of this, since the trade balance is made up of a quantity effect and price effect. Thus even if the quantity of oil falls it is possible that this is offset by a rise in its price. If the impact of North Sea oil on the balance of payments is declining and the non-oil deficits are getting larger, then the fact that the UK possessed this major resource, it is argued, did not require it to tackle some of its underlying problems. The revenue appears to have been used partly to pay for increased unemployment and social security benefits, to reduce taxes and to purchase overseas assets, as Table 10.5 indicates, rather than for tackling the UK's underlying structural weaknesses. Although the UK appears to have been most successful in investing in foreign assets, this may well have been to the detriment of British industry. But what will be the effect on the UK economy when the oil runs out, since it is a finite resource?

As the oil runs out, the process of deindustrialisation may have to be reversed as resources are switched back from services to manufacturing to pay for renewed imports. However, markets once lost are difficult to re-enter and, given the fact that UK manufacturing may have opted out of the middle-quality technology areas, concentrating on low-skill products or on niche markets, there must be a case that over time UK workers and industry will lose the skills sufficient for them to re-enter this middle section of the market on the scale that may be required. Of course re-training may be the answer, but the UK cannot be said to have the best record in Europe. In this case, unless firms completely internalise the costs

TABLE 10.5
International Comparisons of External Assets[1,2]

End-years	1980	1981	1982	1983	1984	1985	1986	1987	1988	1989
United States										
$ bn	95	130	126	78	-8	-122	-285	-389	-542	-675
% of GNP	3	4	4	2	–	-3	-7	-9	-11	-13
% of exports[3]	35	44	47	30	-3	-43	-97	-114	n/a	n/a
Japan										
$ bn	10	10	24	36	74	129	179	240	291	292
% of GNP	1	1	2	3	6	8	9	8	10	11
% of exports[3]	6	5	13	19	37	50	65	66	n/a	n/a
West Germany										
$ bn	26	24	26	27	36	46	90	162	203	254
% of GNP	3	3	4	4	6	6	9	13	17	19
% of exports[3]	12	11	12	14	19	17	26	39	n/a	n/a
United Kingdom										
$ bn	30	53	59	72	87	110	151	134	140	174
% of GNP	6	11	13	16	23	21	26	20	16	21
% of exports[3]	20	41	50	61	81	70	101	84	83	87

NOTES
[1] Excluding gold holdings.
[2] The date underlying this table are taken from national sources which may use disparate methodology.
[3] Gross exports of goods and services.
SOURCE *Bank of England Quarterly Bulletin* (November 1989) p. 521 (November 1990) p. 492.

of re-entering lost markets, there is a case for direct government intervention. By encouraging private direct investment overseas, as Table 10.5
indicates, it could be argued that the government has to a certain extent
reduced the upward pressure on sterling and provided an alternative source
of overseas income to replace the loss of oil. The problem here is one of
ownership. Can we expect the decisions of the private sector with regard
to their investments overseas to be the best ones for society as the oil
revenues deteriorate, and do they conflict with the view of government?

The impact on the UK economy as the oil runs out will be different
depending on the exchange rate regime in use. In a floating exchange rate
system the value of the pound should depreciate and this would allow UK
manufacturing to become more price competitive. Leaving aside the non-
price factors and the elasticities of demand, the UK should find that export
volumes increase. Conversely, import prices will rise and this will feed
through to inflation, wages and interest rates and may lose the competitive
advantage that a depreciation in the currency could bring. Contrary to this
view is the suggestion that sharp changes in the exchange rate cannot
easily be accommodated because of labour market rigidities and that disequilibrium will occur in many markets over the long term. Under a fixed
exchange rate system, the balance of payments will deteriorate in the short
term since it is unlikely that UK manufacturing will respond quickly
enough, and this will force either a devaluation of the currency or push up
interest rates to attract foreign savings. The latter will surely have a
damaging effect on investment confidence. Perhaps there is one positive
fact that can come to our assistance, and that is that oil production will not
simply collapse overnight and the decline may be fairly gentle, giving UK
industry some time to react to changes in the market.

Growth Policies for the Twenty-first Century

The previous chapters, and this one in particular, have highlighted many
of the policies that have been taken to stem the decline of the UK and to
stimulate its growth. As we can see, there is no one solution to the UK's
problems nor is there a group of easy solutions. Moreover, it is unlikely
that the rise of the UK, if it is to come, will be rapid. None the less, there
are conditions in place which suggest that there is some hope for improvement. But the first step is to to determine where the UK wishes to go. Does
it want to resurrect its manufacturing sector or concentrate on services;
does it want to produce the things that other countries produce; or does it
want to move into alternative markets?

For a mature country to raise its rate of success in its use of innovation
may be more difficult than for a developing country, simply because of

sclerosis and institutional inertia. None the less a starting point clearly is education. The UK needs to establish both a workforce and a set of managers who are more adaptable, have higher levels of training and are more appropriately trained. It is too easy to say, 'let us impose the German training system on the UK'. Countries differ in their needs, but more wide-spread vocational education and training perhaps provides a better basis for cumulative learning than a system that relies on employer-based training. To some extent the government may have begun to move in the right direction, stimulating the further education sector whilst at the same time establishing a whole range of training programmes developed through the Training and Enterprise Councils (TECs). R&D expenditure needs to be increased since there appears to be a link between it and subsequent sales revenues relative to those of competitors. Some would go as far as to say that the problem for the manufacturing sector is one of control; there is an unhealthy dominance by accountants over technologists. Others see the problems as marketing barriers to entry for products, especially in the areas of quality, after-sales service etc. Thus the move by UK firms to look at total quality management suggests that they are moving in the correct direction. Alternatively, some firms could be selected in the UK as product leaders to re-establish the UK's reputation for high-quality products on the backs of which other companies can expand their sales in the future. Has Europe's technology policy helped the UK? A report published in 1992 suggested that the impact on Britain had been 'mostly positive', though some would see this as negligible. This highlights that some activity for the UK, however, is European-driven and could be pushing UK enterprises as well as European ones into a more isolationist senario. Firms could be deprived of competitive pressures which are necessary for long-term survival.

The UK system of financial backing and sources of finance is one of the most open in the world. This encourages mergers and takeovers as means of company growth and at the same time satisfies shareholders' demand for quick, short-term profits which some see as damaging the UK's long-term manufacturing performance. In Germany, the financial system gives greater weight to longer-term performance, allowing the benefits from investment to accrue. It is more likely that this divergence between the two systems will converge in the future due to the opening up of financial markets under the SEM regulations which could place UK industry in a better position.

This openness that pervades the British economy could be to its benefit in terms of FDI. The success of the UK in obtaining FDI, especially from Japan, will result in some manufacturing sectors moving from net importers to net exporters during the next decade. Moreover, UK industry has not always sat idly by, some of it has been driven out of the market but other firms/sectors have been stimulated to raise productivity, eliminate overmanning and cease to tolerate low quality. Some argue that if other European countries persist in supporting their own national champions their inefficiencies will put UK industry in a stronger position in the future.

On a macroeconomic level, one of the reasons for the success of Germany and Japan has been the establishment of a financial framework of low inflation, low interest rates, a belief in the consistency of government policy, low government borrowing and a stable exchange rate. If the current fillip experienced by UK firms following the UK's depreciation of sterling after leaving the ERM is not eroded, as on other occasions, by higher inflation, then a few more pieces fall into place to secure long-term improvement in the UK's industrial performance.

On the other hand, a comparison of the growth rates in Germany and the UK suggests that vocational training has played an important part in the better growth performance of the German economy, and the improved growth performance of the UK economy during the 1980s could be linked to a reduction in overmanning and a more efficient use of resources. Whether this means that there was a sudden burst of 'catch-up' rather than a more continuous process is open to question.

A more interesting question is: do we really want a return to a more manufacturing-based economy? For the developed economies the share of manufacturing in the economy as a proportion of GDP has fallen. In 1991 it accounted for 20 per cent of the US's GDP and a similar figure for both Canada and the UK. The argument that a strong manufacturing sector is required so that the service sector can feed off it understates the size of the service sector, since many jobs that are categorised under the heading of manufacturing are really service-type jobs. Thus in looking at the ways in which we can improve the functioning of the manufacturing sector we should not overlook ways in which we can improve the service sector. Perhaps we are already seeing this in the UK with the shakeout of jobs in the banking and financial services sectors. The argument that by switching to a more service-orientated economy productivity levels fall may be an overstatement of the situation, since productivity levels in the service sector are notoriously difficult to measure. None the less, if we upgrade the productivity level of economies because the productivity level in services has been understated then we must do this for all economies. Can the UK rely on the surplus on the service account to offset the deficit on manufacturing? The OECD forecasts for the UK are for the service account to move into deficit early in 1990s. This may be a little premature but it does indicate that the UK has experienced a general downward trend in its surplus on this account.

So where does all this leave the UK? There does not appear to be any one explanation of the poor growth performance of the economy. In fact it is possible to come up with many theories, a view that is supported by economists with the phrase: 'There are more questions without answers.' Of equal interest is the question that, if there was a Thatcher miracle, why did it affect only the manufacturing sector in terms of productivity growth whilst for the non-manufacturing sector there appeared to be no productivity breakthrough, although it was notable that the slow down in UK productivity levels in this sector was less than that for other countries? Moreover, the view that productivity growth rates change counter-cyclically with the level of economic activity appears to be a singularly British phenomenon. Such an occurrence is not to be seen in either Sweden or Japan. Furthermore there are doubts on an international level as to whether productivity measurements in different countries are truly identical.

To wish for a return of the manufacturing sector to aid the growth process is one thing; for it actually to occur is another. The leak of a confidential report from the Department of Trade and Industry in March 1993 indicated that Britain's manufacturing industry was now uncompetitive to a degree that will take decades to rectify. In the short run we may have to rely on the service sector and in particular on the sale of international services, the level of which may be enhanced following the satisfactory conclusion to the GATT Uruguay Round. Moreover the supply-side changes discussed in Chapter 6 are more likely to give long-term cumulative effects rather than a rapid improvement in UK growth.

Can the UK Achieve a Permanently High Growth Rate?

It is easier to suggest in theory why some countries have lower growth records than others, but when it comes to explaining whether this is backed up by empirical evidence we get conflicting views. As Manning notes: 'The empirical results ... give us a clue why identifying the sources of growth may be very difficult. ... much of growth is identified as "catch-up" (A. Manning, reply to N. Crafts, *Economic Policy*, no. 9 (1992)). This is not a complete explanation of the process of growth as it begs the question why there is any catching-up to do in the first place. What it really says is that the factors that cause growth today may have to be sought in the distant past. For economists used to testing hypotheses using econometrics this is bad news; it is implausible to believe that we are going to identify the relevant factors.

But we must be able to start somewhere. Technical progress and capital investment were seen, in Chapter 5, as providing half of observed economic growth, but determining the factors that drive these is more difficult.

Even if we recognise these factors, can we leave it to the market mechanism to provide the 'correct' conditions, as the New Classical school would suggest, or do we require direct government intervention, as advocated by the Keynesians? In the case of the former, direct state intervention is abhorred since it creates greater fluctuations in the economy than would a market-orientated system. Moreover, government involvement was inherently inefficient and led to the crowding out of private-sector investment. Conversely, the Keynesian view is that the government needs to be active in the economy since there is widespread market failure.

In fact, there appears to be a degree of truth in both arguments. During both the periods of demand management of the 1960s and 1970s and through the more *laissez faire* approach of the 1980s Britain's record on R&D and capital investment was relatively poor. Part of this can be blamed on the structure of companies in the UK whose shareholders have desired large short-term profits, much of which could be obtained more easily from investments abroad. However, the conditions for high levels of investment in the UK have not been good, due to the government's policy of squeezing inflation out of the system through high nominal interest rates. If we couple this with a poorly trained workforce we have a further ingredient to explain Britain's malaise.

We are just beginning to understand theoretically and empirically the mechanisms behind economic growth and much further work needs to be undertaken. But this book has highlighted a number of salient variables. There appears to be a strong relationship between investment, particularly human capital investment, and growth. Other factors we need in place are political stability, well-defined property rights, capital investment, low trade barriers and low government consumption activity. Even supposing we have all these pieces in place, it will still take some time before the country sees the benefits of these changes. We need to consider whether we want short-term bursts in growth or whether we are willing to wait for the long-term results from today's policies.

The first step is to recognise the issues, and there is reason to believe that the UK has gone a long way down this road through supply-side changes. However, given the UK's record on long-term investment, will future governments be able to wait long enough for the results before attempting short-term measures to safeguard their political future?

Index